BIOMETRICS
FOR
NETWORK SECURITY

Prentice Hall PTR Series in
Computer Networking and Distributed Systems
Radia Perlman, Series Editor

BIOMETRICS
FOR
NETWORK SECURITY

Paul Reid

PRENTICE HALL PTR
UPPER SADDLE RIVER, NJ 07458
WWW.PHPTR.COM

Library of Congress Cataloging-in-Publication Data

A CIP catalog record for this book can be obtained from the Library of Congress.

Editorial/production supervision: *Patti Guerrieri*
Cover Design Director: *Jerry Votta*
Cover Design: *Nina Scuderi*
Cover art: *Phil and Jim Bliss*
Series Design: *Gail Cocker-Bogusz*
Manufacturing Buyer: *Maura Zaldivar*
Acqusition Editor: *Mary Franz*
Editorial Assistant: *Noreen Regina*
Marketing Manager: *Chanda Leary-Coutu*

 © 2004 Pearson Education, Inc.
Publishing as Prentice Hall Professional Technical Reference
Upper Saddle River, New Jersey 07458

Prentice Hall PTR offers excellent discounts on this book when ordered in quantity for bulk purchases or special sales. For more information, please contact: U.S. Corporate and Government Sales, 1-800-382-3419, corpsales@pearsontechgroup.com. For sales outside of the U.S., please contact: International Sales, 1-317-581-3793, international@pearsontechgroup.com.

Company and product names mentioned herein are the trademarks or registered trademarks of their respective owners.

Printed in the United States of America

First Printing

ISBN   0-13-101549-4

Pearson Education Ltd.
Pearson Education Australia Pty., Limited
Pearson Education Singapore, Pte. Ltd.
Pearson Education North Asia Ltd.
Pearson Education Canada, Ltd.
Pearson Educación de Mexico, S.A. de C.V.
Pearson Education — Japan
Pearson Education Malaysia, Pte. Ltd.

BHR
RPR
JLR
KLR
DRR
JJ
PK
MS
SAR
2Sons
+Sunshine
=Who I am

About Prentice Hall Professional Technical Reference

With origins reaching back to the industry's first computer science publishing program in the 1960s, and formally launched as its own imprint in 1986, Prentice Hall Professional Technical Reference (PH PTR) has developed into the leading provider of technical books in the world today. Our editors now publish over 200 books annually, authored by leaders in the fields of computing, engineering, and business.

Our roots are firmly planted in the soil that gave rise to the technical revolution. Our bookshelf contains many of the industry's computing and engineering classics: Kernighan and Ritchie's *C Programming Language*, Nemeth's *UNIX System Administration Handbook*, Horstmann's *Core Java*, and Johnson's *High-Speed Digital Design*.

PH PTR acknowledges its auspicious beginnings while it looks to the future for inspiration. We continue to evolve and break new ground in publishing by providing today's professionals with tomorrow's solutions.

Contents

Foreword

Biometric technology drives the future direction of strong authentication. The promise of biometrics to protect your data and safeguard your identity from being stolen is very compelling. Like any technology, it has needed time to mature and find its place in the computing infrastructure of enterprises. The time for biometrics has never been better. The industry and technology have matured, and the applications of biometrics are growing every day. From replacing the need for password authentication to strongly binding your physical and digital identities, biometrics is being put to work.

Simply knowing that you need to use biometrics and having read about its use may not always prepare you for deployment. What makes this book special is that it not only explains what biometrics is, how it can be used and the selection of biometric technology but, most importantly, it also explains how to get it deployed.

Paul has many years of real-world experience with biometrics. He explains the lessons he has learned and the best practices that he follows in simple and clear terms. Paul has taken these experiences and consolidated them into two insightful examples that clearly show how using his methodologies will make you successful, as welll as what happens if the methodologies are not used or fully followed.

Biometrics is ready for use and can make the enterprise computing environment more secure. The time has never been better to embark on a more secure way of doing business and protecting your identity.

Tom O'Neill
Senior Partner at Sandler & O'Neill Partners

Preface

Biometrics is fascinating! Imagine having the ability to take a physical trait, quantify it, and then use it as proof of who you are. The excitement I feel about this subject is the same as how I felt when I got my first computer. Here is the latest in technology, and it's mine to explore. It is not often that one is presented with an opportunity to work and research a subject that both excites and has practical applications.

The promise of biometrics has never been greater. With the proliferation of passwords and the need to find a better and stronger factor of authentication, biometrics offer a solution. The use of a biometric trait to replace an existing password or the use of a biometric trait as an access key to Single Sign-On that can then proxy a password is the "killer application" that is going to drive biometrics. The biometric trait provides convenience with increased security. It is exactly this relationship between convenience and security that will drive biometric adoption.

The biometric technologies currently being sold and deployed will make the online world a more secure and private place. For everything that biometrics is and promises to be, it is important to remember it is a technological tool. Like any technological tool, if used for its intended purpose, it performs well; if used where it does not belong, it can fail.

The rate of biometric research is increasing every year. New and more exotic methods are being conceived to measure physical traits. The final chapter goes into more detail on what the future has in store for biometrics.

I believe that the maturity of the biometric industry is in the area of logical security. It is in the protecting of logical access to computing resources that biometrics will make the jump to a mainstream technology. It is with this belief that I took a job at a small biometrics start-up in early 1997. At that time, the industry was still forming for securing logical access through biometric use. There were many companies looking for the right combination of software and hardware to take the industry to the next level. For the next several years, I was privileged to be intimately involved in the development of both hardware and software for this biometric marketplace. It was my role to be the customer-facing resource for the company. I was on the frontline, walking with our customers on the "bleeding edge" of the industry. Being on-site with the customers and seeing how they actually wanted to use the technology gave me great insight into the direction the technology needed to go to be successful. On the frontline, I also experienced the successes and failures of proofs of concept, pilots, and deployments. Along the way, I got screamed at, called at all hours of the day and night, and told that my technology will cost someone his or her job!

It is exactly this "school of hard knocks" approach that has prepared me for writing this book. And it is the culmination of these experiences that I used to compile the book's material.

In any technology field, there are skeptics. It is the skeptics who keep the biometric industry honest, and skeptics can also make the best customers. At a trade show, I was approached by a group of senior technology people from the federal government. They stopped briefly to look at our booth signage and commented about another company with lots of claims and no substance. In talking with them, I came to learn that they had previous experience with a company that had made promises, but never delivered. I explained to them what our company could do and only what we could do, and they said our claims seemed even larger. I offered to demonstrate the solution, and they believed that I would show them "demoware" or make an excuse about why something did not work. On the contrary, I was able to show the full system running and doing exactly what I said it could do. No excuses needed! This federal government group later became a customer. It was this experience that made it clear that if you say you can do something, you need to prove it. It was this encounter that convinced me that when dealing with customers or anyone else, you need to show what you are talking about and deliver on those promises.

It is with that same attitude that I wrote this book. As mentioned earlier, what follows is based on my own experience. It did not happen to a friend of a friend, and it is not some tired, retold case study from years ago. What follows is the truth on implementing biometrics for network security.

Acknowledgments

To get a book to market takes many people doing different things. First and foremost, you need an editor with a vision of what is taking place in the computing industry to see the need to address a new area of technology or innovation. Prentice Hall is a company that has a very good editor in Mary Franz. She showed me that I had the knowledge, the understanding, and the passion to write such a book. On behalf of myself and my family, I thank Mary for all she has done.

I also thank Noreen Regina for keeping my chapters organized and my reviewers' comments in order.

To bring a book to market, it needs to be reviewed. I have been privileged to have Warwick Ford, Manfred Bromba, and Salil Prabhakar review this book for me. It was their comments and suggestions that improved the book immensely. Thank you to everyone for helping me.

Over the years, I have learned that the first step in learning is to understand what gaps there are in your knowledge. By identifying these gaps, you can look for people and resources to help you fill in the gaps. I have been very fortunate over the years to have been surrounded by a large number of people willing to help enhance my learning process.

In particular, I need to thank Larry Hamid and Bob Hillhouse for their time and patience in explaining to me the inner workings of biometrics and smart cards. Without their initial patience and willingness to share their knowledge, I would never have been able to start down this technology path. Thanks, Larry and Bob!

Thanks also to Steve Borza and Gino Vechio for taking the time to fill in my knowledge gaps on integrated circuits, optics, and the manufacturing process. Their many years of experience and hands-on teaching gave me the knowledge I was missing. Thanks, Steve and Gino!

In understanding an industry, it is also important to understand how that industry functions. Thanks go to Simon Morgan and Scott Ashdown for providing an overview of how the biometric industry works, and also thanks to Scott for a good history lesson on the biometric industry itself. Thanks, "Old Man" and Scott!

To enter into a new technology field takes foresight and a belief that the technology has value and purpose. A thank you goes to Wally Rouche of Dew Engineering for having the vision and belief in the technology to start the American Biometric Company. Thank you, Wally.

To reach a point in one's career to have the confidence and knowledge to learn new technologies and then share them with others requires having the right mentors. I have been blessed in my life to have had four of the finest.

Growing up, my father always encouraged me to learn and explore. With support from my mother as well, I continued my exploration and learning of computers. It was this early experience that created my desire to learn new technologies and gave me the confidence to master them. Mom and Dad, thanks!

The second mentor I had was John Jed. He taught me that the best way to learn was by doing. He also provided the balance between technology and rest of the world. He taught me that the most important things in life come down to "Good friends, good food, and good times." Thanks, John!

I was also lucky enough to find, during one of my earliest jobs a, seasoned veteran of the computer industry named Pierre Kerr. "PK," as we called him, had been around computers since the early days of time-sharing and punch cards. It was while I was working with Pierre that he taught me that many of the "leading-edge" technologies today had their bases in previous technologies or industries. It was this understanding that taught me that simply because something is old, it does not mean it is not worth learning or understanding. Thanks, PK!

The current mentor in my life is Marshall Sangster. Marshall, for the past eight years, has shepherded me and my career. Marshall imparted to me the knowledge of how to tie technology to business. He taught me a very important lesson about losing. I always believed that losing was through lack of effort. Marshall believed that if you were not losing occasionally, you were not trying hard enough! Thank you, Marshall!

Even with the great fortune I have had with mentors, I would still not be anywhere if it was not for my wife, Stephanie. When we were married, she did not expect to have a husband who would need to travel to all parts of the world at a moment's notice or be on the phone all hours of the day and night. Through all the time I was away–the late nights at work, the weekends in front of a computer, the missed birthdays and anniversaries–she never complained. It was her never-ending support and love that allowed me to do the things I needed to do, to grow in my career and knowledge in this field. Stephanie and our children, Nicholas, Katherine, and Gregory, have given me the support and love I needed to get this book done. Thanks to them, the book has been completed.

Part 1

INTRODUCTION AND BACKGROUND

1

Introduction

Stop! Right now, think of how many passwords and personal identification number (PIN) codes you have to remember. Now, think back to when you started using passwords and PIN codes. How many did you use then compared to now? For most of us, the number of passwords and PIN codes we currently have is somewhere between 5 and 8. For some, that number can be as high as 12 to 15. How often do you forget them? It is very inconvenient to remember those codes. Now, do you have your fingers, eyes, voice, and face with you? The answer hopefully is yes! Have you ever forgotten any of those body parts? Not very likely! What if we could use those body parts instead of passwords and PIN codes to verify who you are? Would that not be more convenient? It also seems logical that it could be a more secure way of authenticating a person.

Biometric technology uses a physical or psychological trait for identification and/or authentication. By using physical traits, the provider of the trait always has them with him or her.

This book is about using those physical traits for providing access to computers and their networks. *Biometrics for Network Security* is a book dedicated to helping those interested in the use and implementation of biometrics systems for access control to be successful the first time.

This book is based on my own real-world experiences. The methodologies, observations, and suggestions are based on several years of real-world, in-the-field experience. Everything I talk about in this book really happened to me. I did not get the information from a presentation or hear a story secondhand from a friend; I have been in the trenches and have the scars to prove it!

What Makes This Book Different?

As outlined above, it is my real-world experience in delivering biometrics for network security that will differentiate this book from others. You will not find in here the same tired examples used in other books—examples that have been rehashed endlessly as case studies to be learned from. I want to teach you and prepare you for taking on a biometrics project—not only to evaluate the technology and understand it, but to actually get it deployed and thus deliver on the promise that biometrics can deliver.

The Structure of This Book

The book has four sections:

Section 1–Introduction and Background

While this section title is seen in many other books, this book tries to provide a different view. The first chapter in this section is about authentication technologies. If you are to use and deploy biometrics, you need to understand where they fit in relative to other types of authentication, and also where one authentication method may be better than another for a given use. Chapter 3 describes privacy issues. While other books tackle privacy, it is normally from the user's perspective. In this chapter, I contrast and balance the needs of privacy for the employer, employee, and customer with biometrics as both an enabler and a compromiser of privacy.

Section 2–Biometric Technologies

This section deals with different types of biometrics and biometric devices. The devices described in these chapters were selected by me to reflect, at the time, what I believed to be the best suited for network security. Each chapter in this section has the same format so that it is easy to compare one biometric device's features versus another's. Before any discussion on technologies takes place, it is important to define what makes a good biometric for network security and which features of a biometric are most important to evaluate for network security. The final two chapters of this section discuss the mathematics of biometrics and how a complete biometric system can be secured.

Section 3–Implementing Biometrics for Network Security

This section is what truly sets this book apart. In three chapters, the reader is led through the proof of concept, the pilot, and lastly, the roll-out. In the chapters of this section, the stories of Martin and Jason will be told. Martin and Jason personify the right and wrong ways to deploy biometric technology. Martin is the culmination of my experience when the outlined steps are followed and the biometric project is delivered. Jason is the culmination of my experience when the different stages of the methodology are skipped or not taken seriously. It is these chapters that will make or break the success of a project.

Section 4–Future and Conclusions

With the serious aim of the book out of the way, it is fun to try to predict what the future holds in store for biometrics. I have seen some of this technology myself, and can say without any doubt, it carries a high "cool factor."

Everything You Need to Know about Biometrics to Understand the First Three Chapters

Biometrics, like any other technology, have their own nomenclature and acronyms. While these are covered in great detail throughout the book, below is a primer on basic biometric technology and terminology to get you started. What is covered here will be just enough to get you going.

What Is a Biometric?

As mentioned earlier, a *biometric* is a physical or psychological trait that can be measured, recorded, and quantified. By doing this, we can use that trait to obtain a biometric enrollment. This way, we can say with a degree of certainty that someone is the same person in future biometric authentications based on their previous enrollment authentications. The degree of certainty will be discussed in greater detail in Section 2.

Enrollment, Template, Algorithm, and Verification

In a biometric system, a physical trait needs to be recorded. The recording is referred to as an *enrollment*. This enrollment is based on the creation of a template. A *template* is the digital representation of a physical trait. The template is normally a long string of alphanumeric characters that describe, based on a biometric algorithm, characteristics or features of the physical trait. The *biometric algorithm* can be viewed as the recipe for turning raw ingredients—like a physical trait—into a digital representation in the form of a template. The algorithm will also allow the matching of an enrolled template with a new template just created for verifying an identity, called a *live template*. When a stored template and a live template are compared, the system calculates how closely they match. If the match is close enough, a person will be *verified*. If the match is not close enough, a person will not be verified.

FAR, FRR, and FTE

As described above, when a stored and live template are compared, they either match or they do not match. What happens if it is not you who is trying to match to your template? In this case, someone else is trying to verify as you. If that person were to match as you, it would be classified as a *false acceptance*. The probability of this happening is referred to as the *false acceptance rate*, or *FAR*. The FAR normally states, either in a percentage or a fraction, the probability of someone else matching as you. Thus, the lower the probability, the less likely a match. That means that a match needs to be closer to the original template. As the closeness of a match increases, what does this mean for you when you try to verify as yourself? It means that your live template must match even closer to the enrolled template. If you fail to match against your own template, then you have been *falsely rejected*. The probability of this happening is referred to as the *false rejection rate*, or *FRR*. Thus, the higher the probability of false rejection, the greater the likelihood you will be rejected.

Lastly, when you are new to a biometric system and need to enroll but cannot, this is called a *failure to enroll*, or *FTE*. The FTE normally states, either in a percentage or a fraction, the possibility of someone failing to enroll in a system. A discussion in a later chapter will cover the relationship among FAR, FRR, and FTE as it relates to choosing a biometric device and algorithm.

Who Should Read This Book?

This book was written for the network manager or network security manager. There are others who could benefit from reading it. Below is a list of chapters that each particular person in a company would benefit from reading:

- Chief executive officer (CEO)–Chapters 2, 3, 4, and lastly, skim Chapters 12, 13, and 14. These chapters will provide a solid understanding of the technology and its applicability to an organization.
- Chief information officer (CIO)–Chapters 2, 3, 4, 10, 11, and lastly, skim Chapters 12, 13, and 14. In reviewing these chapters, you will be best prepared to talk about and articulate the issues concerned with using the technology and the preparation required for successful deployment.
- Project manager–Chapters 2, 12, 13, and 14. By reading these chapters, a project manager can become familiar with biometrics and the special project management tasks required to deliver a successful biometric project.
- Network administrator or security specialist–Chapters 2–10, and skim Chapters 11–14. This way, the technology can be examined in greater detail and the project management chapters can be left for the use of the project manager.

Conclusion

This book was written to provide a guide and roadmap for the successful deployment of biometrics for network security. The book is broken down into sections to keep the related information contained, and to allow the different groups of people reading this book to get the most out of it.

2

Authentication
Technologies

Everywhere you go, you are constantly identifying and authenticating whomever you see. For example, the way you would identify a friend in a crowded mall is to look for familiar features. Is the person male or female? What color is his/her hair? Is he/she short or tall? Is he/she wearing a familiar piece of clothing? When your friend sees you looking at him/her, that friend may respond by greeting you by name. By using your previous knowledge, you have authenticated that person as your friend. Can we be assured that we have the right person? Probably not 100%, but we have mitigated the risks and come to an acceptable level of comfort with his/her identity.

The above scenario is very similar to what a computer system goes through when a user wants access. Computers should be only accessed by legitimate users. To know if a user is legitimate or not, the computer is supplied with a username and a method of authentication. The most common way to identify a user is through a username or identification (ID). These often take the following forms: last name, last name with first initial, employee ID, or a fully distinguished x.500 identifier. How a user authenticates depends on the authentication methods available.

There are three main ways to authenticate an identity:

1. Something you know, like a password or pass phrase
2. Something you have, like a token
3. Something you are, a measurable trait

These are often referred to as the *three pillars of authentication*. They can be used separately or combined for even stronger authentication. Let's look at each in further detail.

Something You Know

This refers to anything that needs to be remembered to prove your identity. The information remembered could be of the following types:

- Passwords
- Pass phrases
- PINs
- Secret handshakes

Passwords are the most frequently used forms of authentication. Passwords are used to authenticate you with information that only you know. If you supply a computer with the proper password, it authenticates you as a user. Passwords, however, have the following problems: They can be stolen, written down in easily accessible locations, shared, or guessed. To strengthen passwords, they are normally implemented with a supporting policy. Sharing passwords, writing them down, or not changing them frequently violates most password policies. Automated methods can be used to enforce a password policy. The number of days between password changes and the strength of a password can be enforced through an operating system or an application that supports a strong password policy. A strong password policy would include rules like the following:

- A password must be a minimum number of characters in length (e.g., 8).
- A password must include characters of both upper and lower cases.
- A password must contain numeric and non-numeric characters.
- A password cannot repeat any character more than a certain number of times.
- A password can be used only a certain number of days.
- A password cannot contain a substring of the username, company name, or any other easy-to-guess words.
- Insert your favorite esoteric password rule here.

As you can see, a good password is not easy to remember and is difficult to devise. Most people have a hard enough time trying to remember where their car keys are, let alone remembering a password that looks like something that was dropped on a keyboard. So, what do we do if we can't remember something? We write it down, we tell our friends in case we forget, and we don't change it! This password that started out as a strong form of authentication is now an open secret stuck with a Post-it® note on our monitor!

Users do many wrong things with passwords because their passwords are not convenient to remember. Users will write their passwords down on sticky notes on the sides of their monitors. They will even write their passwords and user IDs on their keyboards!

So, it seems that forcing strong passwords on users actually backfires and, in fact, ends up decreasing security. If a user was provided with a simpler password policy, that would weaken the strength of the password. It should, however, provide an easier password for the user to remember.

A weak password policy has the following characteristics:

- The password is short in length.
- Characters of different cases need to be used in the password.
- No numeric or non-alphanumeric characters need to be used in the password.
- Characters may be repeated many times.
- The user never has to change the password.
- The password may be composed of character strings from the username, company name, or something easily guessed.

As you can see, a user should really have an easy time thinking of a password that can be remembered, especially if the user has used a simple password policy. What we forget is that users are human. So, in typical human fashion, they still write passwords down, they share passwords because they are simplified, and they do not change passwords because they can finally remember them!

The much-maligned password does have its place, however. The applicability of a password is more a factor of what is being protected. If I want to restrict access to my address book, a password may be sufficient. If it is compromised, the entries could be changed or exposed with little harm. On the other hand, a critical system protected with a password makes as much sense as picking the word "password" for access.

Passwords seem to provide a paradox. No matter what password policy we choose, the "Barbarians at the gate" could still get in. Maybe passwords do point us in the direction of better factors of authentication. It seems that the biggest obstacle to users using strong passwords is the inconvenience of the password itself. Therefore, the more convenient the authentication method used, the stronger we can make it. This in itself seems impossible. Normally, as user convenience increases, the strength of authentication decreases. The perfect example is the password. If other technologies could be found to give us increased user convenience and increased security at the same time, then we would have the best of both worlds.

Something You Have

Anything that is unique and that the user is required to possess can be used as an authenticating token. A token is generally issued to one user. A token is registered to a user, and when it is presented for authentication, the token is verified as being legitimate. The identifying label of the token is used to verify its registration, if it has been lost or stolen, and if the user ID presented with it matches. If it is a match, the user is authenticated. Otherwise, the authentication request is rejected. Tokens fall into two general categories:

1. Storage tokens
2. Dynamic tokens

Let's examine each in further detail.

Storage Tokens

Storage tokens are generally made up of smart cards and Universal Serial Bus (USB) tokens. There is unique information stored on the token that identifies the possessor. If a computer system accepts only the presentation of a token for authentication, then anyone who has that token can be authenticated. If the token is lost or stolen, entry can still be gained. However, passwords are employed with tokens to prevent this from happening. Thus, when a user wants to authenticate with a token, he/she inserts the token and then provides a password to unlock the credentials stored inside. The token and the password are used by the system to authenticate the user. This *multi-factor* authentication methodology still has the weaknesses of passwords because the token and associated password can be loaned or stolen. Still, simply knowing the password without the token is not sufficient for authentication. Both must be used together. Most people are familiar with multi-factor authentication from ATM use: The card is the storage token and the PIN is the password. That said, the user is still inconvenienced, as he/she needs to remember two things instead of only one: the password and where the token is.

Dynamic Tokens

Dynamic tokens come in many forms, including smart cards, USB tokens, and key fob styling. What makes these tokens different from storage tokens is they are used to generate a one-time authentication code. The code could be in the form of a challenge sent from the computer and the response from the token, or a registration of the token and time-based response keys. Just as for the storage token, the simple possession of a dynamic token is not sufficient for authentication. The dynamic token must be used in conjunction with a password to authenticate. This is still inconvenient for the user.

Token Usability

Tokens do have their use as a method of authentication. Storage tokens are most often used in conjunction with digital certificates. The certificates are stored within the token and then released for authentication. This method is most commonly used for Web-based authentication. It can also be used in Windows 2000 and XP as a certificate-based login, or in a Kerberos environment for granting an access ticket.

Dynamic tokens are most often used for remote access. The user enters the response code from the token into the remote client software along with his/her password for authentication. This method of authentication is gaining market share. It does not require additional connected hardware on a remote personal computer (PC). Thus, a user can go to any Internet-connected computer and strongly authenticate to a company network.

Tokens in conjunction with passwords have brought us one step closer to strong authentication. Still, the strength of tokens is compromised by the need for the user to remember his/her token and the password to access it. Tokens do offer a suggestion to attain a better factor of authentication. This better factor of authentication would have uniqueness like a token, require the user to process it, but not require a password to access it.

Something You Are

Any physical trait that can be reliably measured can be used to authenticate and is called a biometric. Biometric authentication is nothing new. In the opening paragraph of this chapter, biometrics were used to identify someone as a friend. This has gone on throughout history. If someone is authenticated based on some physical trait, then biometric recognition is in use.

Biometrics can be used for *identification.* A user makes no claims about who he/she is. A biometric comparison attempts to match an individual's biometric data against all the biometric data on file. This is what is referred to as *one-to-many matching*. One-to-many matching is used in the law enforcement world. In this use, biometric data is matched against previously stored data in the system. This matching generally returns a set of possible matches. From there, a final determination must be made with human intervention. This type of matching is normally done for physical access or law enforcement applications.

Biometrics can be used for *authentication*. If a user makes a claim about his/her identity, a biometric is used for authentication. The biometric comparison in this case will attempt to match the individual's biometric data to that of the stored information being claimed against. This is referred to as *one-to-one matching*. The result from this matching is a simple yes or no: Yes, the individual's claim is verified, or no, the claim cannot be verified. If the claim cannot be verified, no more results are provided to further narrow down the claim. This type of matching is generally done for logical access or physical access to specific parts of buildings.

Biometrics now seem the ideal solution. The user always possesses the physical trait and a password or token is not required for access. Later chapters will contain more detailed discussions on how strong the different biometrics are, and how susceptible they are to spoofing.

The Need for Strong Authentication

Computer networks and systems have been accessed for many years by passwords. Why now is there a need to have stronger factors of authentication? To understand this, you need to understand the history of network computing.

Network Convergence Role in Password Proliferation

When computing was hitting it big in the enterprise world, everyone who needed computing resources shared a central mainframe. This gigantic piece of equipment acted as the central processing point for all data. Users were connected to it through cryptic-sounding protocols such as SNA, ENA, and BSC. The connection was proprietary and allowed only equipment of the same make to share the network. Thus, if the finance department of a company wanted computing resources, it would jack into the mainframe. All that changed, however, with the advent of the PC. The PC gave every user a dedicated processing unit.

The user could decide what applications to run and never had to worry about time-sharing or queuing up with punch cards. The user was untethered from the mainframe.

A funny thing happened after this. Users realized they had lost the ability to collaborate, or share files and data. People were running "sneaker nets" from one PC to another with 5.25-inch floppies. This was not an effective way to share data. So, these new PC users took a page from the mainframe and networked their PCs locally. Thus, local area networks, or LANs, were born.

Most early LANs used a central server for storage and authentication. Some also had peer-to-peer networking. LANs were connected using, at times, proprietary protocols like IPX/SPX, NetBeui, and Arc-Net. A department's being able to share and store data centrally and share printers made a lot of sense. As the personal computing revolution continued, more and more departments were getting LANs. It was not long before an enterprise would have between five and seven LANs in operation, and quite possibly a mainframe as well. It became clear that disjointed networking was not generating economies of scale. Sure, most of the major LAN providers created gateways to the mainframe, but still, the LANs remained separate. LANs of the same networking provider could share a common network, but what if users needed to have everything connected? This is where the Transmission Control Protocol/Internet Protocol (TCP/IP) came in.

TCP/IP was the saving grace of the enterprise IT department. One network was set up, over which a user could access any resource connected to it. This system then saw a rush of corporate resources to the masses. The IT managers had brought economies of scale to the corporate computing world. What they had also done was create a multiheaded monster. Now an attacker could get access to any system in the network that was connected. Earlier, the attacker had to go from LAN to LAN and physically from department to department. Now, all the attacker needed was a LAN drop somewhere on the inside and an IP address conveniently provided to him/her by the enterprise Dynamic Host Configuration Protocol (DHCP) server. To make matters worse, TCP/IP provided the enterprise with the ability to connect to the Internet. Now that "the little LAN that could" was connected to the Internet, an intruder no longer needed to breach the physical security of the company; he/she could carry out all attacks from the comfort of home.

Passwords in the best of times are weak and, in general, easy to guess. With an enterprise connected to the Internet, the entire computing effort of many connected computers can be used to guess a password with brute force. In brute-forcing a password, every possible password combination is tried. This method exhaustively searches all possible solution sets for a password. What would have taken weeks, months, or even years in the isolated LAN environment can now take hours, minutes, or even seconds to gain access by using the combined computing power of the Internet. It seems that in the rush to bring the corporate LAN to the world and into the twenty-first century, password authentication was made dated and stale.

Mitigating Public Risk through Government Regulation

Because enterprise corporations connect to everyone, everywhere, at any time, the results of any network compromise could be catastrophic. Many important vertical industries are connected today to public networks and are thus being regulated by the government. These include:

Financial institutions

The risks of a breach to the public or an individual could be tremendous. If open market operations are compromised, the cascading effect on the economy could be catastrophic. For example, the malicious buying or selling of currencies on the open market could cause a country's economy to collapse. The theft of private individual data already leads to identity fraud or monetary loss. Thus, many governments are enacting legislation to require financial institutions to implement strong authentication for access to customer data and for many types of financial transactions.

Healthcare industries

The risks of personal data being changed or disclosed for an individual could be catastrophic. If a patient's record was maliciously altered to remove an allergy to a medication or to change a procedure, it could have life-threatening ramifications. The personal medical data about an individual could be used to deny health or insurance coverage, or it could be used for blackmail. Since the healthcare industry contains the most sensitive data about an individual, many governments are enacting legislation to protect access to this data and to mandate the use of strong factors of authentication.

Pharmaceutical companies

For a pharmaceutical company, time to market is money. Finding a process that can be streamlined means that new drugs get approved faster. To accomplish this, many governments are enacting legislation that allows the electronic submission and sign-off of drug testing data. With this streamlining of the process, the possibility of electronic fraud is higher. To mitigate this risk, the government is also mandating the use of graded authentication. Based on the sensitivity of the electronic sign-off, different factors of authentication could be used, including the use of public key infrastructure (PKI) certificates for electronic signature, password protection, smart cards, and biometrics.

Governmental entities

With the majority of world governments using computers, it is not surprising to see the networks they are on under constant surveillance. The public and private information stored in these systems could give an intruder access to the most critical government information, or the opportunity to manipulate the data in the intruder's favor. The personal data of the citizens of a country could be used for identity fraud, changing the government benefits a citizen receives, or tampering with legal matters. In the post-September 11th era, governments around the world are much more vigilante about network and data access. As such, governments are implementing strong authentication for most systems that are deemed sensitive or essential. For example, routers that used to be protected with static passwords are now using challenge and response tokens, or one-time passwords. Network access to sensitive data is now controlled with multifactor authentication.

Military organizations

The Internet was originally created by the military and other U.S. government organizations to make it easier to share data. With the whole world now connected, it is very easy for enemies of the state to attack and try to compromise this connected infrastructure. As such, the military is implementing strong authentication for computer networks. In the U.S., the Department of Defense (DoD) has undertaken an ambitious program of issuing millions of smart cards for both physical and logical access. It has also created internal organizations to investigate biometrics and their use in network security. The DoD continues to lead the rest of the computing world in the use of strong authentication.

With the possibility of personal data being released, the risk of tampering with corporate data, or the malicious use of connected resources, the government has seen fit to regulate many of these verticals. These regulations mostly deal with how the data is to be used, stored, transmitted, and, most importantly, accessed. The regulations being put into place do recognize the need for stronger authentication. This recognition is normally tied to a specific set of data, or the access to sensitive information. The regulations will list, in order of increasing assurance, what factors of authentication are acceptable. For example, a common listing may look something like this:

- Password
- Password and token
- Biometric
- Biometric and token
- Biometric, token, and password

It is interesting to see that one factor of authentication, a password, is considered weaker than another factor of authentication, namely a biometric. It is generally accepted that a biometric is a stronger means of authentication than a password. As we saw earlier, biometrics in general cannot be stolen, loaned, or guessed. The spoofing of biometrics will be covered in more detail later. For the purpose of our discussion, it is *certis paribus* that there are more successful methods of attacks on passwords than on biometrics. It has been shown that passwords are susceptible to dictionary attacks and also brute-force attacks. A biometric, on the other hand, by its very nature is hard to subject to brute force. For the ultimate in assurance, three-factor authentication should be used. The probability that combination of something you have, something you are, and something you know will be compromised is very low. Still, this high level of assurance does lessen user convenience.

To summarize, if a vertical industry itself does not self-regulate, the government is prepared to do it.

Mitigating the Risks from an Inside Threat

To avoid government regulation, industries need a strong authentication plan. It may be not only to appease the government watchdogs, but also internal ones as well. Corporate risk management is flexing its corporate muscle more and more each day. Tasked with minimizing risk in the operations of the business, corporations are now looking closely at the risks associated with information technology (IT). They need to protect the enterprise from:

- Internal threats
  - Rogue employees conducting unauthorized transactions
  - Corporate espionage
  - Data tampering
  - Compromise of client data
- External threats
  - Network intrusion
  - Corporate espionage
  - Data tampering

Most of these threats can be mitigated through other means like intrusion detection systems, auditing, trace files, and forced employee holidays. Most internal threats come down to authentication and non-repudiation. The need for non-repudiation in business is not new. For decades, business was done face-to-face or via paper agreements. Now, in the age of email and the Internet, business is conducted faster and with a larger group of partners and suppliers. For example, when an agreement is made or a letter sent, I affix my signature to it. If I could do the same in the electronic world, I would have my non-repudiation, or would I? In the real world, all those involved normally sign an important document, and those signatures are witnessed. We could use this same methodology electronically and have people witness my electronic signature with theirs. This could give a stronger assurance that the desired person really did sign the electronic document in question. But, if electronic signatures are not strongly authenticated, how can we be sure, as the recipient of such a document, that all signatures are legitimate?

Corporate IT can provide end-users with the infrastructure and tools to certify the authenticity of electronic signatures. The recipient of an electronic signature could check the certificate revocation list to see if the electronic signature is still valid. However, once we know that a signature is valid, we are still not assured that the owner of the electronic signature was the one to actually use the electronic signature. To be sure that the owner was the one to affix the electronic signature, we first need a strong way to authenticate the user. If we rely on passwords, then our digital identity can be loaned, stolen, and, in general, compromised. If we tie that digital identity to a smart card, the card and password can be compromised. So, as the recipient of a signature, I still cannot be sure if the owner of the digital identity, or someone who has the card and password, signed it. But what if we put the digital identity on the smart card and protect it with a biometric? Now, as the recipient of a digital signature from an individual, I can be sure that the individual was present. This assurance comes from the electronic binding of the smart card containing the digital signature to the owner's biometric. The digital signature can be affixed to the document only if the owner presents his/her biometric to release the signature from the smart card.

The Role of Strong Authentication with Single Sign-On (SSO)

We have seen how biometrics eliminate the need for passwords or digital certificates. By removing the need to have a password, we increase both security and user convenience at the same time. This at first glance seems to be a paradox. Normally, if you increase security, user convenience decreases, such as when implementing stronger password rules. Conversely, if you decrease security, user convenience increases. For example, you would probably surmise that when users have weaker password rules, they are no longer inconvenienced because they can pick an easy-to-remember password. But, we have seen that this is not the case. No matter what password rules are used, user convenience and security suffer. This inverse relationship is best illustrated with an application of biometric authentication used in conjunction with single sign-on (SSO).

SSO has been the promised Holy Grail for end-users for many years. One of the greatest weaknesses of SSO is that access to all credentials is protected by a weak method. Historically, SSO software allowed a user to have his/her credentials proxied. To access this credential store, the user would present a password that unlocked the secret store and made it available. Thus, if the user picked a weak password, the whole secret store could be compromised. If the user picked a strong password, the amount of convenience from the SSO was traded off against the difficulty of remembering the password. Thus, the user would write the password down and/or share it. This gave SSO a bad reputation, but in reality, it was authentication technology that was not where it needed to be.

Today's authentication technology has caught up to SSO and many vendors are currently offering strong authentication options to be used in conjunction with SSO. If a user could strongly authenticate to the secret store, could the SSO software, in turn, not use stronger passwords? Some of the better SSO packages offer the ability for the software to randomize the stored credentials. Thus, the user no longer needs to remember a password as he/she strongly authenticates, and the passwords provided by the secret store are now stronger because they are randomized. SSO seems to provide to biometrics the "killer application" that every new technology needs to make it mainstream. In our case, mainstream is the corporate enterprise.

Biometric Technologies: An Intelligent Solution

Everyone always wants the latest and coolest stuff, and this holds true for the computer industry. Many firms eagerly jump into the next big technology so they can say they were there first. This is referred to as being on the leading edge. In recent times, many have believed that biometrics were not on the leading edge, but on the bleeding edge. The bleeding edge is where a technology gets debunked. Biometrics have spent more time than any other technology in recent memory on the bleeding edge.

To a large degree, the biometric industry has been its own worst enemy. Early on, the biometric industry made grandiose claims about the ability of biometrics to authenticate and secure. Many claimed no FARs in the hundredths of millions. Many claimed they could not be spoofed, and that they could enroll anyone. At the same time, the public believed biometric technology to be the "snake oil" of this century.

The truth falls somewhere in the middle. It was true that early biometrics were really nothing more than bright, shiny tools. Lots were sold, one and two at a time, but none was really put into production. At the same time, the industry kept improving the designs and driving down the price. Biometric systems started to get academic scrutiny, and with it came external verifications of claims. Those whose claims could not be substantiated were quickly found out and passed over. Those with realistic claims and expectations continued to seed the marketplace. In recent years, there has been a maturing of the industry and the charlatans and pretenders have been weeded out. What remains is a solidly mature market from which to select biometric solutions.

The procurement of biometrics for strategic corporate research is a good thing, as long as the research group is aware of the limitations and uses of biometric technology. For example, at a busy airport, it might not be prudent to use a finger biometric to check the identities of everyone passing through. This would be too slow, as each person would need to make physical contact with the reader. Facial recognition would work better, as passengers could be screened when entering or exiting a plane. On the other hand, a corporate network security environment is best served by a biometric that is easy to use and widely accepted. In this case, employing a finger biometric is an appropriate and intelligent choice.

Conclusion

Whether authentication is being done for verification of a friend's identity or for computer access, the same factors of authentication can be used. Something you know, something you have, and/or something you are can be used to provide increasing levels of assurance of your identity. If we combine these factors, we can achieve even better results. The drive to interconnect the corporate desktop PC on a LAN and the subsequent connection to the Internet have provided access to vast computing power over the Internet. This computing power can be used to compromise passwords in a fraction of the time it used to take a single computer. Consequently, passwords are now a larger security risk than ever before. At the same time, users have more passwords to use and remember. Strong authentication can provide better authentication methods than passwords. The strengthening of an electronic signature and the convenience provided by SSO are made possible through the use of biometric authentication. The move to stronger authentication is being driven by password proliferation and network risk mitigation. Employing biometric technology is an intelligent part of any strong authentication strategy.

3

Protecting Privacy with Biometrics and Policy

The encroachment by technology into individual privacy has never been greater. From being tracked by surveillance cameras as we travel through cities and businesses to the use of customer loyalty programs, our movements and habits are under constant surveillance. The lack of personal anonymity is decreasing quickly as more personal information is gathered about us. This gathering and tracking can begin as soon as we turn on our cell phones in the morning. The cell phone puts out a "here I am" signal to the nearest cell phone towers. Using the strength of the signals at each tower, your location can be triangulated. On the drive to work, you may have a transponder in your car, to whisk you through the toll lanes on the freeway. Now there is a record of when you passed a certain location. When you park and take the train into the city, the cameras of the transit company have you under surveillance. They can tell with whom you sat, what newspaper you read, and at what station you departed. As you exit the train on the way to work, you may stop at a pharmacy and get a prescription for high blood pressure filled. While there, you pick up some potato chips for your children that night. You pay for your purchase and use both a credit card that lets you get points for purchases and the pharmacy's loyalty card. The pharmacy now knows that you bought a prescription and snacks. This information, if sold to your health insurer, could form the basis for the insurer to think that you are not doing what is best for your high blood pressure and personal health. From the pharmacy, you head to work; you pass the security gate, where you present your photo ID, and then enter camera-monitored hallways and elevators to get to your desk.

23

During this trip to the office in the morning, your every move and action have been tracked and recorded. During this trip to the office, only twice have you positively identified yourself. The first time was when you signed your credit card receipt at the pharmacy, and the second time was when you presented your photo ID at the security checkpoint. All the other times, you have been watched and quite possibly recorded as an anonymous face. If any of the surveillance cameras that captured your image had been integrated with facial or gait biometrics, you could have possibly been identified. It is the possibility of a third party identifying you without your consent or knowledge that is of greatest concern.

Privacy is really much more than the personal information we think of. Privacy can apply to anything that we want to keep private. In keeping something private, we wish to safeguard it from use or view. For example, meeting with different people or organizations could be seen as personal matters. I may also want to keep my physical person private. That is, my body is private, and I should expect privacy in not being viewed intimately. The thoughts in my head are private to me, and if I wrote them down in a journal, I would want that to remain private. Thus, I would expect others to respect the privacy of my thoughts. The right to or need for privacy must be protected somehow. The protection afforded my information is of importance. If I am required to share certain private details with my employer in order to be employed, I expect my employer to protect the privacy of that information. The use of a password is one way to guard the privacy of my information; requiring biometric authentication to access that data would be even stronger. In this way, biometrics help to preserve my privacy. If my employer were to use facial biometrics for authentication, I would be enrolled in the system so I could authenticate at work. If my employer used that biometric information to identify me outside of work, or to correlate my movements with those of others, my privacy would be violated, as my right for privacy with whom I meet would be invaded. In this way, biometric identification technologies are seen as invaders of privacy.

With employers now looking at using biometrics as a strong factor of authentication, all the previous prejudices concerned with the loss of privacy need to addressed. The right to privacy and the expectation of it are not only individual concerns, but also concerns for employers and employees. Biometrics play a role in each group's privacy issues and concerns. Biometrics can be seen as both a compromiser of privacy and a protector of that privacy. Once the role that biometrics will play in each party's privacy is clear, it is important to try to create a positive biometric policy in order to ensure that the rights of both the employer and employee are protected. Let's examine each group's concerns about privacy and biometrics and use this discussion to provide an outline for a positive biometric policy.

Employer's Right to Privacy

Employers are usually incorporated and, as such, they have some of the same rights as individuals in society. They can sue and be sued. They can enter into contracts and conduct business in their own name. In the same way, they have a right to privacy. For an employer, the privacy issue is more than who knows what; it is also about the use of private company resources and facilities. The access to a company's resources and facilities may provide a mechanism by which the company's privacy can be compromised. The implementation of biometrics by an employer or its employees can help control privacy issues in a number of ways. What follows are some of the areas in which a company can use biometrics to ensure its privacy:

- Protection of trade secrets and proprietary information
- Protection and safety of employees and customers
- Background checks
- External reporting and auditing requirements
- Access control

Let's examine each in more detail.

Protection of Trade Secrets and Proprietary Information

Many companies value their trade secrets and proprietary information more highly than their capital resources. These corporate secrets give them a competitive advantage in the marketplace. If these were to be compromised and exposed publicly or to a competitor, it could have catastrophic results for the company, employees, and shareholders. This is equivalent to an individual's wanting his/her personal thoughts to remain private.

Consider, for example, a publicly traded cola company. If the secret recipe for a cola was compromised, then competitors could imitate the flavor, and it might allow market fringe players to gain a larger market share. The loss of market share would cause a decrease in share price, reducing company equity and shareholder value. As the stock price falls and the revenues decrease, the company may be forced to lay off employees and reduce expenditures. This would have multiple effects in the economy. With less money being spent by the company, and a loss of spending by the laid-off employees, tertiary businesses would be affected.

This compromise of corporate privacy is an issue for all interested parties. The root cause of the invasion of privacy was the lack of access control to the trade secret. The trade secret could have been stored on a computer server, on a network, or in a secure location. Access to it was either controlled through password authentication to the network or by key card to the secure area. As we saw in Chapter 2, the password is a weak factor of authentication for a number of reasons, and simple possession tokens are not a strong enough factor of authentication on their own. To strengthen the privacy of a company's trade secrets and proprietary information, the employer could employ a biometric for network authentication. This would help ensure that the person authenticating to the network is the one who should or should not have access to the sensitive information. If a biometric was used for physical access to a restricted area of the company, then only authorized employees would be able to access the data stored there. This use of biometrics is easily justified due to the importance of the data being protected. An employee objecting to using a biometric for access control holds less significance than the rights of the employer, employees, and shareholders protecting their monetary interests. In doing this, the privacy of the company's "thoughts" is better safeguarded.

Protection of Personal Data about Employees and Customers

In today's litigious environment, a corporation is not only expected to protect itself, but also its employees and customers. The corporation is expected to safeguard customer information from unauthorized access and tampering. At the same time, employees have expectations that the confidential information collected about them will be treated with privacy.

For a customer of a healthcare provider, the information stored with the provider could be used maliciously against the customer. This is an example of privacy of the physical person. I may need to share certain private physical health information for insurance. Thus, there is an expectation that the information provided will be treated with the utmost concern for privacy. If the privacy of the individual is not respected, the following could happen with an invasion of privacy:

- Denial of insurance coverage due to pre-existing conditions or family history
- Denial of employment based on a disability or medical preconditions
- Threat of exposure of a medical procedure or condition
- Removal or addition of medical conditions that if treated or untreated could cause illness or death

The customer expects the healthcare provider to take all necessary steps to safeguard this information. Using biometrics would help to mitigate the risk to the customer. If biometrics were used for authentication to the database containing the customer data, the healthcare provider would be able to control and audit who accessed the data and what changes they may have made. Once again, the public good that using a biometric device would provide would negate any employee objections to the use of biometrics.

For an employee of a corporation, protecting the data gathered about the employee is of great importance. The type of information that an employer may have gathered about an employee due to his/her employment may include:

- Background and criminal histories
- Previous employment history
- Current address and contact information
- Bank account information for direct deposit
- Current health coverage
- Web surfing activities
- Email correspondence
- Salary information

The exposure of any of the above information would infringe on the privacy of the employee. The employee would thus have an expectation that the company would treat access to this information in the same manner as customer data. Here again, the use of biometric devices can help insure that this information remains confidential. Access control and auditing can once again be meaningful if the people accessing the data are biometrically authenticated. The privacy rights of employees who access the data stored about other employees and customers need to be second to the privacy rights of the employees and customers to whom the data applies.

Background Checks

Before we would invite a total stranger into our home, we would want to know more about him/her. We would try to find out as much about his/her background as we could. This may give us some indication of what to expect from the stranger currently and into the future. In the same way, a corporation will want to know about the background of any potential employee before hiring him/her. This would afford the corporation the opportunity to either reject him/her as an applicant or hire him/her being well aware of his/her background. These background checks have historically involved letters of reference, follow-up phone calls to references, and police checks. All the checks conducted rely on the applicants being truthful about his/her identity and providing legitimate credentials as proofs of identity. A dishonest applicant could easily provide false information and credentials. The applicant may be trying to hide previous employment with the company or previous criminal activity.

In recent times, many corporations have been using ink fingerprinting to validate identity and, in turn, using these fingerprints for criminal background checks. This method requires taking accurate prints and shipping them off-site for verification. Both could result in time lags that could give the candidate, if hired, the ability to commit a fraudulent act.

The use of a biometric device that generates Automated Fingerprint Identification System (AFIS)-quality images can reduce the time of a background check and will tell you immediately if the image is usable. In this instance, the use of the biometric not only protects the corporation, but also speeds up the applicant's hiring process. All parties concerned benefit from this use of biometrics.

An applicant may be concerned that the biometric data collected for this purpose could be subverted for other uses, or shared with others. If the applicant was not successful or was not hired, would the biometric data collected be destroyed? For the corporation, it would be in its best interest to keep this data to deter the unsuccessful candidate from re-applying and current employees from committing illegal activities. In this case, both the employer and the candidate or employee have reasonable privacy concerns. How to address these will be dealt with later in this chapter.

External Reporting and Auditing Requirements

Employers often have private information about their business activities or other non-public information. Company employees, in conducting their jobs, can use this private information. However, if this private information was used for other means, it would be an invasion of the employer's right to privacy. This invasion of privacy may have consequences to third parties. To know if this has happened, the employer may need to have reports and audits done to detect the wrongful use of the private information. As such, governments and other licensing bodies have imposed reporting and auditing requirements on corporations. These requirements are mainly put into place for the safeguarding of privacy and to prevent the exploitation of insider information. To meet these requirements, corporations are quite often required to:

- Provide separation of data
- Provide accurate transaction reports
- Provide internal memos and emails

A detailed description of how biometrics can help achieve the above follows.

Provide separation of data

In many corporations, there could be an internal conflict of interest based on the data collected and the activities that the corporation is involved in. For example:

- A financial conglomerate that acts as both an investment bank and an open markets trading company—The information that the investment bank part of the company has access to could provide a trading advantage to the open markets portion of the company.
- A healthcare conglomerate that offers both insurance and healthcare delivery services—The delivery side of the business could feed back to the insurance side new or pre-existing health conditions that could result in the loss of insurability or an increase in premiums.
- A utilities producer that is also a reseller and market maker for the utility it produces—The market maker side of the corporation could have knowledge of a plant's going offline or a new supply's coming to the market before it is publicly known. The producer side of the company could restrict additional capacity during a peak consumption period, thus causing prices to spike and larger margins for the produced capacity.

In each of the examples, the requirement for separation of data can be accomplished with biometrics. With biometrics controlling access to the data, only the properly accredited employees would have access to create or read the data stored. It could be argued that if the properly accredited employees do have access to the data, or change the data and then share it verbally with the other side of the company, this would then give the company an unfair competitive advantage. In this case, biometrics do not prevent this exchange from happening, but biometrics can provide the "smoking gun" for what took place. If the individuals involved are confronted with their actions, the non-repudiation property of biometrics would prevent them from denying their actions. The access to the data and the subsequent activities based on knowing the data could be tracked back to the individuals involved based on their biometric authentication. For example, imagine the following scenario from the financial sector: An investment banker biometrically authenticates to get the latest sales forecasts for a customer. He/she then has lunch with a trader friend and shares the latest sales data. The trader later authenticates to the trading system and trades the security. Both cannot deny doing their parts in the fraudulent activity because of the biometric authentications.

Provide accurate transaction reports

When an employee conducts an activity as part of his/her job function or on behalf of the corporation, an accurate record should be kept. This record needs to indicate the following:

- Who performed the transaction?
- What was the transaction?
- Where was the transaction conducted?
- When was the transaction executed?

Biometrics can help provide support for each of the above.

Who performed the transaction?

With a biometric authentication, there is never any doubt about who performed a transaction. The employee would have authenticated to activate the application. A subsequent authentication can be performed to commit the transaction. In this way, the user's name is bound to the transaction record. If a digital signature is in use at the company, then the digital signature would be affixed to the transaction as well.

What was the transaction?

A transaction record could be changed after completion. If this happened, there could be a question of what really took place. If a biometric authentication was required to access the transaction log, that access and activity would be recorded, along with the biometric authentication to make the change. In this case, biometrics can be used to protect the integrity of the record after a transaction has been recorded.

Where was the transaction conducted?

Sometimes the location where a transaction took place can be of importance. The location may be used to prove collusion between two parties, or that the transaction was illegal based on government regulation. The transaction log would record the IP address of the computer from which the transaction was executed. If the application transaction log was compromised, the biometric authentication log file could be used to provide the proper IP address. In this scenario, the biometric authentication creates a unique log file on the biometric server that records the address of the computer and the application that requested the authentication.

When was the transaction executed?

Like the previous example, the timing of a transaction can be important. The time of a transaction can prove when the information in question was used. In the case of information being used before it was publicly known, it can prove insider knowledge. As in previous examples, the biometric server authentication log can be used to validate transaction time.

Provide internal memos and emails

With the scandal-ridden collapse of numerous corporations and the many accusations of insider trading, an electronic paper trail is more important than ever. The internal memos and emails of a corporation are like an individual's thoughts. They are written down and may be shared with others in trust. The privacy of these "thoughts" needs to be protected.

Internal emails and memos have brought down many empires and have put previously untouchable corporate executives in jail. Many defense lawyers could argue that the accused never actually sent an email or wrote a memo. In turn, the prosecution will want to show that the accused authored the correspondence. Both would benefit from biometric authentication. If the accused was required to biometrically authenticate to send correspondence, it would show that he/she did or did not send a certain memo or email. To have a stronger case, it would be best if the email or memo was digitally signed and the signature could be used only if it was biometrically authenticated. In this case, the combination of digital signature and biometric authentication would prove innocence or guilt.

Access Control

It is clear from the employer's perspective that privacy concerns are best addressed when biometrics are used for access control. The further upstream a privacy breach can be prevented, the better. The earliest point in most cases to prevent a privacy breach is at the point of authentication. If we can insure that only the proper employees have access to their required information, employer privacy can be safeguarded.

Employee's Right to Privacy

The employee's right to privacy and the employer's need to protect its corporate interests have always been at conflict. Early on, employees were treated like property. Once in the employ of a company, the corporation controlled many aspects of the employee's life. It wanted to know with whom the employee associated, to what organizations the employee belonged, the religious affiliation an employee held, and other aspects of the employee's personal life that could affect the company. The advent of trade unions and other such groups did much to remove these intrusions into the employee's everyday life. Today, the employee is facing a number of privacy issues that never before existed or were of little interest to the employer.

Protection of Personal Data Collected by the Employer

Not long ago, an employee's personal file contained relatively little information. The most confidential piece of information contained in the file was the employee's social security number. The government required this number so that taxation could be applied to the employee's salary. In today's data-rich world, most employees would be surprised to see what information their employer has about them. This information could include:

- Credit history
- Medical coverage

- Insurance and beneficiaries
- Criminal history
- Photo of employee
- Ink fingerprint card
- Phone numbers called from employer's phone system
- List of bookmarked Web sites
- Voicemails
- List of Web sites surfed
- Daily arrival and departure times from place of business
- Electronically stored biometric data

The simple fact that this data has been collected can be very unsettling to an employee. The employee would be rightly concerned over who is viewing this data, and what it is being used for. As discussed in the section describing the employer's requirement for privacy, biometrics can be implemented to help enhance the privacy of the employer. When biometric systems are in place, they can be used by the employer to help protect the employee's privacy. However, the same biometric that is helping to protect the privacy of the employer and the employee could also be used to invade the employee's privacy. What follows next is a discussion of the impact of biometrics on the privacy of the employee.

Biometrics as an enabler of employee privacy

Employees do have a concern over who can view the personal information collected about them. Biometrics can help in this area. If the information about an employee is stored electronically, we can use biometrics to protect access to this information. This way, only other employees who have a requirement to access this information could do so. It would also deter the employees who have access to this information from sharing it with others. If the employees with access to this sensitive information know that they can be positively identified as accessing other employees' confidential information, they may be less likely to provide this information to a third party or gossip about what they know.

Physical access biometrics can be used to prevent unauthorized employees from gaining entry to securely stored paper records. If a biometric authentication is required to access paper documents, it will deter unauthorized access and help manage required access. It should also give the employee some sense that the company is doing what it can to safeguard personal data.

Biometrics used to invade employee privacy

An employee needs to be made aware of what personal information is being collected and what it is being used for. Most employers have the legal right to monitor what an employee does in conducting business on behalf of the employer. The employer has the right to monitor how corporate resources are used. The employer may listen to employee phone calls and voicemails. The employer may do this to determine with whom the employee is communicating. The employer may hear personal information being communicated at the time. This information could then be stored or recorded for future use.

The employer may use digital surveillance cameras to watch for unauthorized access. These cameras can record digitally and their output can be stored indefinitely. A group of anonymous employees meeting in a hallway and talking may not be of any interest to an employer. However, if one of the employees in the group turns out to be supplying information to a competitor, the employer may want to know to whom they were speaking.

Many companies now require an employee to submit to a background check. These background checks are mainly carried out using fingerprints. The employer collects the prospective employee's fingerprint images digitally and sends them off for a background check. The number of industries doing this type of checking has increased since September 11, 2001.

Without even realizing it, an employee may give the employer a sample of his/her biometric traits. Voicemail or recorded conversations can be used with voice-based biometrics. Digital surveillance cameras can provide both face and gait biometric information. Lastly, the collection of a fingerprint can be used for fingerprint biometric verification. There are really two issues here that are of concern for the employee. First, the biometric data collected for use with voice, face, and gait biometrics could be obtained without the employee's consent or knowledge. Second, how is the employer going to use the biometric data collected?

Collecting employee biometric data can be done either covertly or overtly. In an *overt* collection of biometric data, the employee knowingly submits to the collection of data. In a *covert* system, the employee does not know about his/her biometric data collection. In the cases of voice, face, and gait data collection, the employee may not be aware that the employer was collecting this data. The employer could argue that the surveillance cameras are visible and well-known, that the employee should not have the expectation of privacy while at his/her place of employment. With the collection of fingerprint biometric data, the employee knows that it is being collected. The employee needs to be present and actively submit his/her finger for fingerprinting. In this case, the employee knows that the biometric data is being collected for a background check.

The second, more invasive problem is, what other uses does the employer have for this data? An employee can never know for sure, but the company's privacy statement can give some indication of how the data will be used. In general, the privacy statement should make mention of disclosure policies for third parties. Some policies say that for business or legal reasons, private information may be shared. The policy will often go on to state that any third party will abide by the same privacy statement as the company releasing the data. It may also say that the company releasing the data is liable for the third party's misuse of the data. This can be reassuring, but who monitors whether or not the third party breached its agreement? It is generally the responsibility of the company that shared the data originally. It would be in the company's best interest not to find any breaches, as it would be liable for them. Thus, you have self-regulation that does not really work.

What is an employee to do? The best an employee can do is to be diligent in how his/her personal information is used and provide only the absolute, bare minimum. Be aware that your personal data is a valuable commodity. Any interaction you have with an entity that is not tracked is a lost opportunity for data gathering. The lost opportunity can be seen as possibly lost revenue if sold, or lost intelligence on the employee.

The real onus of providing a positive biometric privacy environment falls on the company. It is the company that wants to use biometrics to enhance its authentication. If a company wants to use biometrics, it must create a privacy policy that respects the employee as an individual, yet at the same time affords the company a strong factor of authentication.

Creating a Positive Biometric Policy

The largest obstacle to overcome in a successful biometric implementation is user acceptance. A user will not accept biometrics for any number of reasons. These could include fear, ignorance, stigmatism, religious beliefs, and the loss of privacy. A pro-privacy policy statement can address the user's concerns. The policy statement should address the following areas:

- Biometric enrollment
- Template storage and transmission
- Verification
- Terms of use and audit statement

Let's expand on each in more detail.

Biometric enrollment

A privacy policy must clearly state what biometric are being enrolled and how data will be captured. A pro-privacy policy will allow only biometric enrollment through overt means. This means that both passive and active biometrics will be taken only with the user's full knowledge and consent. Passive biometric measures like face, voice, gait, and to a lesser extent, eye-based biometrics can be taken from the user without his/her knowledge or consent. A camera in the lobby could record a person's face and/or gait. A camera in an elevator by the floor selection panel could read retina and iris biometrics. A microphone in a hallway or elevator, or the user's phone handset, could be used to record a voice biometric. In all these cases, the user would never know that his/her biometric had been enrolled. It is paramount that if these types of biometrics are used, the user is clearly told when they are being enrolled to allow him/her to consent to the enrollment.

Active biometrics like finger, hand, and vein biometrics require the user to actively submit to enrollment. These types of biometrics would be seen as more privacy-friendly. At the same time, the user still needs to be made aware that he/she is being biometrically enrolled in order to allow him/her to consent to the enrollment.

The enrollment portion of a pro-privacy policy statement should also clearly outline that what is about to take place is a moment of trust. The enrollment agent or someone else of authority must positively identify the user being enrolled. The greatest risk of fraud in a biometric system comes at enrollment time. The user must be prepared to produce appropriate documentation and/or have other trusted parties in the company vouch for his/her identity. It should be made clear that this is being done for both the protection of the employee and the employer. From the employee's perspective, positive identification means that he/she will be the only one claiming to be him/her when the biometric system is used. This way, if a biometric audit log is used to verify who did a particular action, the employee knows he/she will not be falsely identified.

When biometric enrollment takes place, the company needs to disclose the following regarding the enrollment:

- Is it compatible and comparable with law enforcement databases?—There are a number of reasons why an employer and employee may/may not want to have a template compatible with existing law enforcement databases. From an employer's standpoint, having a template that is compatible gives the employer the chance to find out if there is an employee with a criminal background. It can also allow for a third party's verification of the employee's identity. This verifying for positive identification can prevent previously terminated employees from re-applying. It can also stop individuals from using pseudonyms or other means of identity fraud. From an employee's standpoint, being positively identified will prevent others from trying to be enrolled as him/her. This form of identity theft would be detrimental to an employee in that the employee could be associated with activities he/she did not commit.

- The need for re-enrollment—Over time, biometric measurements can change. If the biometric system being used does not in some way account for these changes, the number of false rejections for an employee will increase. This increase in false rejections will cause frustration on the part of the employee and diminish the expected results of the system for the employer. Biometric re-enrollment needs to be explained to the employee. The employee needs to understand that his/her stored biometric data will eventually deviate too far from the template to be usable. At this point, the employee will be asked to re-enroll. Re-enrollment from the employee's perspective will continue to offer him/her the ease of use initially obtained from the system. It gives the employer up-to-date templates to use for comparison. This will also lower the number of calls to the help desk about false rejections.

- Is the biometric image stored or is a template created?—The end-result of a biometric enrollment is the capturing of biometric data. The form in which biometric data is stored is important to both the employee and the employer. This biometric data can be stored in its raw form, or turned into a template. The raw form of the data is the biometric measurement before it is processed. This could be an image of a finger, face, iris, or other traits. It could be a raw .wav file for voice. This is the data that would be fed into a templating algorithm.

- The current state of biometric technology today does not require raw data. All biometric systems work from templates. The keeping of raw data is useful only for applications like face verification. The raw image could be stored along with the template. When the user authenticates, a guard viewing the stored raw image could make a secondary verification. This obviously benefits the employer and does not really invade the employee's privacy. Unless the employee is walking around with a mask on, the face is one biometric that is always visible. The storing of a fingerprint image is normally of more concern. Many believe that the raw image could be used to spoof an authentication system or make a fake finger. As we will see in a later chapter, the creation of fake fingers is possible. Therefore, it is preferable to have the raw biometric data discarded and a template created.

- A template created from raw biometric data should contain enough data for verification, but not enough data to recreate the raw biometric. Templates are normally created using a one-way hash algorithm. The algorithm takes the raw data, extracts the information it needs, and then processes it. Once the raw data is processed, there is no way to go back. The use of hash functions is covered in greater depth in a subsequent chapter. When a biometric comparison needs to be made, the newly acquired image is put through the same one-way hash function as the original biometric enrollment. This way, it is this template that gets used for comparison.

Template storage and transmission

When an employee is being biometrically enrolled, templates need to be stored somewhere. Templates can be stored in relational databases, in smart cards, as files on a user's computer, or in a corporate lightweight directory access protocol (LDAP) directory. The employee's and employer's privacy concerns are different depending on where the template is stored. For discussion purposes, let's group the storage of templates into locations. LDAP directories and relational databases are network-based and are thus available online; local files and smart cards can be considered offline storage.

Privacy concerns with templates being online are:

- Online storage is controlled by the employer
- How templates are retrieved for comparison

Each point needs to be examined from both the employee's and employer's perspective.

- Online storage is controlled by the employer, so the management of online storage is a privacy concern for the employee. The employee's biometric data is no longer under his/her control. The employee no longer has the ability to allow or deny access to this data. In addition, the employer has the template available at any time. This way, the employer is the final arbitrator of who has access to the data, and with whom it is shared.

- From an employer's standpoint, the responsibility of controlling biometric data is very important. This repository needs to be under control in order to assure the employer of the validity of the data. If this data is compromised and is used outside the company or for other nefarious purposes, the company could be held liable. On the other hand, having the data under the employer's control allows greater flexibility in its use. Depending on the nature of the agreement between the employer and employee, the biometric data could be used in conjunction with other data to put together a complete employee picture. This could include things like time and attendance, travel patterns in the buildings, time of lunch breaks, and other sundry information. This information could be used to better manage the employee, or could be sold to third parties.

- How templates are retrieved for comparison–For a biometric authentication to take place, a biometric sample needs to be taken. The new raw biometric data is put through a one-way hash function and a comparison template is created. The comparison template is then compared against the reference template stored online. The retrieval of this template can pose privacy concerns for the employee and employer. Ironically, both parties have the same privacy concerns, but for different reasons. Employers are always concerned about compromising the templates for fraud and unauthorized access. Employees are concerned over identity theft.

For both parties, the security of online template storage is important. Online storage in either a relational database or an LDAP directory has similar properties that cause concern. Both have the following characteristics:

- Access control lists (ACLs) are required
- Network-based resource accessible companywide

- Accessible through TCP/IP or other networking protocols
- High on the "hit list" for hacking

ACLs are security mechanisms that are applied to records in a relational database or attributes in an LDAP directory. The ACLs control who can read, write, delete, or make changes to records themselves. These ACLs can be set for individual users or groups, or they can be inherited from higher up in their access tree. ACLs have the potential for privacy invasion if they are not set and managed properly. One of the biggest failings with ACLs is the over-assignment of rights. This over-assignment of rights normally occurs when there are problems with accessing certain data. Instead of analyzing why the data cannot be accessed, the administrator will keep on granting higher levels of rights until access is achieved. In doing so, the administrator may inadvertently grant access to information that should not be made available to everyone. This can cause the template to be accessible and might lead to its compromise. The proper way to handle this is to assign the ACLs with a minimum amount of privileges. If the templates need only read and write access for the users, then the users do not need delete or other properties concerning the ACLs themselves. Also, the ACLs for templates should be set through group ACLs. This way, if a server or a new administrator needs access to the templates, they can be added to the group. And, if an administrator no longer needs access, he/she can be removed from the group, and not as an individual.

When templates are stored on a network-based resource, they are network-accessible. This way, it would be possible for almost any machine in the firm to reach their storage location. Networks can be partitioned and routing can be disabled to different subnets, but if you need to have free seating, then you cannot limit where a user can access these templates. A better solution would be to have a trusted proxy between the requests for templates. This trusted proxy would be the only means of accessing the templates. It would be better still if the actual matching of the templates took place on a trusted server. This way, the server could also act as the proxy and return a template only to itself. Using this approach, the templates would never leave the trusted server, and on the server acting as the proxy, the templates would have the appropriate ACLs for access. The only flaw in this solution is that database or LDAP directory that is being used for template storage could also be used for other applications. These other applications may require that end-users directly access the database or directory. So, even if the templates have the proper ACLs on them, unauthorized access attempts can still be made. For example, there are well-known attacks that can be carried out on databases and directories for unauthorized access. The fact that these do exist demands that the security group of a company make every effort to keep the network secure and the data repositories patched with the latest fixes from their vendors. This way, the risk may be mitigated or reduced.

The economies of scale that corporations have reaped from implementing TCP/IP have also proved to be a security risk. TCP/IP is the networking protocol that allows everything to be connected and share the network infrastructure. TCP/IP is what allows corporations to connect to the Internet, send and receive email, browse the Web, and offer applications and data for use by partners and customers. This TCP/IP network is also the one that lets the attackers and hackers right in the company's front door. As discussed in Chapter 2, TCP/IP provides the mechanisms for these attacks to occur. This, combined with the templates being stored by network-based resources, provides the opportunity for compromise. Again, protecting the templates from being compromised is part of the network security group's responsibility. If access to the templates is compromised either from the inside or the outside, the templates can be posted and moved around the world in fractions of a second. The sheer computing power available on the Internet could then be put to work for compromising the templates. The simple fact that the templates have left the control of the employer is in and of itself cause for concern. The connections between the template repository and the verification location can also be cause for concern. There are TCP/IP hacker attacks that can be used to receive the packets destined for the proper recipient. These attacks allow hackers to access the packets or interact with the application listening on the server. Proper operating system choices, applying all the operating system and application patches, and good security models in the biometric software can help alleviate these risks.

The network-based resources in which the templates are stored are high on a hacker's target list. Databases and directories contain information that others would probably want. As such, they are frequent victims of hacker attacks. Since they are such highly valued targets, large numbers of hackers try out the latest exploits to compromise these systems. As such, the probability that the servers where the templates reside will have well-known attacks is high. It is imperative that the servers that hold the database or LDAP directory be secured both physically and digitally. These servers should be on the inside of the firewall, and not host any applications or services that would require external connectivity. These simple security practices will reduce the risk of external attack, but they may still be vulnerable to an internal attacker. Most security intrusions are either perpetrated by an insider or with the assistance of insiders. As such, the greatest weakness once again is the human condition.

While biometrics provide a means to mitigate some of the human risk, they cannot mitigate all of the associated risk. Good human resource (HR) and IT policies can also address the insider threat. HR policies can stipulate that unauthorized access to corporate resources, or the disclosure of company information, is a punishable offense. IT policies can force administrators to follow best practices and mandate the rotation of personnel to prevent fraud from being perpetrated for extended periods of time. Personnel rotation is very common in the banking industry. The idea behind it is that employees in all positions either rotate out of their positions or have mandatory holiday time. This time away is meant to prevent the ongoing cover-up of illegal activities. An employee cannot cover up his/her actions if he/she is not present. This works well, assuming that the employer has a way to check on illegal activities, or suspects something.

Verification

Once an employee is enrolled, the reference template is used for verification. The privacy concerns of verification are as follows:

- Reason for verification
- Where the verification match takes place

Let's examine these verification concerns in more detail.

Reason for verification

Like any factor of authentication, a request for verification should not be taken lightly. When an employee verifies, he/she is confirming his/her identity with a high level of certainty. This creates a point of recognition. The employee is no longer an anonymous entity. The employee now has an identity and associations can be made. If the verification is done in the course of doing company business, then it is a justifiable verification. If the verification is frivolous or intended to create non-business-related associations, a breach of privacy has taken place. Examples of justifiable verification are:

- Physical or logical access to a company building, resource, or computer network
- The binding of a physical person to a digital persona

- Proof of identity before conducting private transactions
- Proof of identity for employment reasons

Examples of unjustified verification are:

- Verification for access to non-critical resources or facilities
  - Washrooms
  - Fitness centers
  - Cafeteria
- Passive biometric verification
  - Security wanting to know the name of an anonymous face for personal reasons
  - Wanting to know the names of people smoking outside the building
  - Associating a name to a person carrying shopping parcels from a particular store
- Access to non-corporate Web sites

What are the reasons behind justifiable and unjustifiable verifications?

Justifiable verifications

- Physical or logical access to a company building, resource, or computer network—As an employer, I want to make sure that access to my buildings and resources occurs only for authorized employees. To accomplish this, I require every employee to verify his/her identity before entering or accessing a building or resource. This is justifiable since it takes place while the employee is discharging his/her duties. The employee has no justifiable grounds to deny verification. It is part of the employee's employment to use these resources or access these facilities. As such, the employee must be expected to provide all reasonable accommodations to me as the employer.
- The binding of a physical person to a digital persona—As seen in Chapter 2, one of the reasons for biometric deployment is to provide a physical binding between your digital identity and your physical one. A digital certificate in and of itself is worthless unless tightly bound to an individual. Once this binding has occurred, it is only fair to assume that use and access to the digital certificate would require verification. The employer will want to know for certain that the employee was the one who electronically signed a transaction. This way, the employee

must provide the verification to fulfill the security vision of the company, and also to ensure that the recipient of the transaction/email received it.

- Proof of identity before conducting private business—In the course of being employed, there are a number of times when an employee needs to identify who he/she is. These authentication requests could be for access to HR, for medical reasons, or for employee benefits. Ensuring the confidentiality of employee data is the responsibility of the employer. Requiring an employee to authenticate him/herself to get access to data is justifiable.

- Proof of identity for employment reasons—As outlined earlier, an employer wants to verify that an employee or potential employee is who he/she says. To achieve this level of certainty, the employer will request of the employee a verification of identity. This could be in the form of a background check to verify criminal history. The verification could be used to prevent discharged employees or previously rejected candidates from seeking employment. It could also be used to prevent fraud of the same person receiving salary and/or benefits multiple times under different names. In this case, the employee or candidate has willingly offered services for employment. As such, the employee or candidate must be willing to accommodate this justifiable request for verification.

Unjustifiable verifications

- Verification for access to non-critical resources or facilities—While the needs of employee verification for physical and logical access to corporate resources are justifiable, not all resources or facilities should require verification. If access to all corporate resources or facilities mandated verification, the perceived value of that verification would be diminished. For example, if an employee needed to verify for access to trade secrets or corporate financial information, that same verification should not be required to use the washrooms. This diminishes the importance of verification for trade secrets and corporate financial details. These justifiable verifications lose their effectiveness and come to be viewed as just another bureaucratic activity.

  In the same vein, verification for access to resources like washrooms, health facilities, and cafeterias seems intrusive. A concerned employee could view the interest in the employer of positively identifying the individual as nefarious. This perception of nefarious activity could lead the employee to believe that the employer is using a moment of recognition as an opportunity to correlate data about anonymous users. This correlated data could then be sold, or used internally, without the user's consent. For example, being able to put an identity to a face that uses the health facilities every day may identify a prime candidate for targeted mass mailings from fitness companies. Also, the knowledge that this particular individual uses the health facilities, makes six figures, and has a wife and three children adds increased value to this information for sale to marketing groups. At the same time, an employee who regularly eats at the cafeteria and orders from the grill line, and is never seen going to the health facilities, could be "red-flagged" for additional health screening for insurance re-qualification. As you can see, the above examples of verification are not justifiable when viewed in the context of discharging one's corporate responsibilities.

- Use of a passive biometric—One of the biggest privacy fears for an employee is not knowing when he/she is being watched. One of the factors that mitigates this concern is the general anonymity an employee has while moving about. If the employer uses passive biometric systems, however, this anonymity is decreased or lost. The employer can establish a moment of recognition whenever he/she needs to. These additional moments of recognition could occur for non-business reasons. An example could be a security guard wanting to know the name of an employee so he/she could ask the employee for a date, or worse. Another example is a company that has less life insurance coverage available to employees who smoke. Thus, it would be in the company's best interest to be able to identify employees who smoke. In today's work environment, smoking is an activity that does not occur in company buildings; smokers are forced to go outside to designated smoking areas. This provides prime locations for passive verification to take place. The employer can control where these smoking areas are set up and the lighting and access ways to these areas. These factors provide an ideal environment in which to create a moment of recognition. Now that the employer knows who smokes, he/she can use it for internal reasons; the employer could also use it to provide direct marketing information.

The marketing data which a company holds on an employee is quite often seen as an untapped revenue stream. In tough economic times, normally scrupulous companies sometimes do the wrong thing. For example, the value of knowing which employees are married, have children, and earn a particular amount of money is pretty lucrative in and of itself. Now, if the employer can correlate this static information with new dynamic data, the value of the marketing data can soar. For example, a corporate location near a major shopping center can provide the company with such information. Many employees may run errands or shop during their breaks. The employees may bring procured items back to their place of employment. When an employee shops somewhere, the store often gives a bag to carry purchases in. The bags are usually emblazoned with the logo of the store. This information, when combined with a moment of recognition, can correlate all the data together. This is clearly an unjustifiable use of verification. Not knowing and controlling when these unauthorized verifications take place can only diminish the amount of privacy and anonymity an employee has.

- Access to non-corporate Web sites–With the advent of the Internet being as commonplace in business as the telephone, companies has provided policies to ensure proper use. A *proper use statement* generally comments on the type of content that is allowable for viewing, what the Internet connection can be used for, and what applications cannot run across the company's link. To better secure and speed up Internet access, a company may implement proxy servers. To "control" access to the Internet, authentication is required to the proxy server. This moment of recognition can be used to correlate the sites visited after verification with a particular user. Again, this illustrates how the static data that an employer has about an employee can increase in value with correlation. If a user seems to be spending a lot of time looking at car sites and the latest car reviews, he/she is probably a pretty good candidate for a car loan or purchase. If the moment of recognition happened only when the user wanted to access corporate sites and resources, this would be justifiable. But, using moments of recognition to further increase the value of the data stored on an employee is unjustifiable.

Where verification takes place

The act of verification is purely computational. Wherever there is sufficient computing power, a verification could take place. Historically, biometric verifications take place on:

- Servers
- Workstations
- Smart cards

Let's examine each in more detail.

Servers

Server matching seems to offer the ideal solution. The match takes place away from the client and on a machine that is in a secure facility. This server is, to a large degree, considered trusted. It has not been physically or logically compromised. When the reference template is used for verification, it is never exposed to the PC in any way. The software on the client machine making the request is expecting back a simple yes or no answer from the server. Assuming the communications between server and client are secured, the server solution is ideal. The reference template is never exposed and the authentication can be automatically audited.

One of the drawbacks of using servers is the problem of how employers can support offline users. The obvious answer is they cannot with server-based authentication only. This leaves two other choices: Use the user's workstation/laptop or use a portable token like a smart card.

Workstations

Using workstations for authentication provides location convenience. In general, the user will always have access to one and will normally carry a laptop if traveling. The use of a workstation creates additional concerns, however. These additional concerns are the inherent distrustful nature of workstations and how templates get to the workstation for verification.

Workstations in general are not to be trusted. Employees can load almost any software they like on them. They will modify and change security settings on their workstations because the security administrator granted them full access so as not to have any access-denied issues.

Workstations and laptops tend to be lost or stolen at an alarming rate. The storage of templates on any local machine is a concern if a laptop is compromised. Most biometric solution providers have a mechanism to get templates to a workstation. Once there, they are stored and encrypted until needed for verification. Thus, the templates can be attacked continuously if a laptop is stolen or compromised. A better solution would be to age the templates and then delete them. An *aged template* is one whose continued access has been blocked by some means. An aged/blocked template could be reactivated if the workstation talks to a server online or has the aged template reactivated. Aged templates are securely deleted from workstations after a predetermined number of days. This way, a thief or attacker has a limited timeframe in which to access the templates.

Smart cards

Smart cards have been used historically for stored value purchasing and lately for more logical access requirements. Smart cards are great. They come with their own processor and memory. The speed and size of the smart card chip dictate the type of processing of which the card is capable. With biometric verification, a match using a smart card can occur on the card if the biometric vendor supports a match on the card. A variation of this is to create a comparison template on a PC, then send the new comparison template to the smart card. The smart card does the comparison and then returns a yes or no. If the return is yes, then the user is verified.

Smart cards also contain reference templates. The biggest benefit of the smart card is the secure storage of the templates. For someone to hack a card, he/she would need access to it, and would have to have a very detailed understanding of the card's structure and operating system. With a smart card system, the employee gets offline access to applications and the employer gets secure storage of the templates.

Terms of use and audit statements

The terms of use and audit statements in a positive biometric policy should define the following:

- What can the biometric data be used for?
- Will it be used in correlation with other data?
- Length of storage of the biometric data
- Audit trails for access to the biometric data
- Audit trails created from verification
- How the employer is audited against terms of use
- Will biometric data be shared with third parties?

- What options do employees have who cannot or will not use biometrics?

Let's expand on the above points

What can the biometric data be used for?

Once an employer has possession of biometric data, it should be clear from the terms of use of the positive biometric policy when and how it will be used. It should clearly state when biometric verifications will be required and how the results of the verifications will be used. It needs to state the requirements the employer will put on the employee for re-enrollment and any other possible uses.

Will it be used in correlation with other data?

This part of the statement will give the employee some idea of what other uses the employer has for the data. If the employer is going to correlate verifications against other data, the employer needs to clearly outline what this new combined data will be used for. If it is to be used for third-party disclosures, the employee, by default, should be able to opt out of this. Any exposure of correlated data to a third party for uses other than the core business of the employer should be clearly defined. No employee should have as a condition of employment the sharing of his/her data with third parties other than for core business reasons. The employee should also have the right to view all data that has been correlated against moments of recognition.

Length of storage of the biometric data

The employee has the right to know how long the employer intends to keep the employee's biometric data. The length of time should be reasonable to ensure the employer sufficient protection, and at the same time, the employee should have confidence that the data will be properly disposed of. A positive biometric policy should outline the number of days, weeks, months, or years the data will be kept in case the employee leaves, is dismissed, retires, or dies. The policy should also state how the data will be destroyed, and if any data correlations will also be destroyed.

Audit trails for access to the biometric data

The employee has a right to expect that only authorized business access will take place with biometric data. To ensure this, audit trails must be kept. An audit trail should show enrollments, deletions, modifications, time last accessed, and time last accessed by user ID. This way, the employer is forced to examine the logs for its own protection. If there is evidence of illegal activity, the employer could be held liable for any damages an employee incurs.

Audit trails created for verification

When a user is challenged for a moment of recognition, there must be an audit trail of this event. The audit trail needs to show the location of the request, the date and time, the application that requested the authentication, the challenged username, the FAR, and if the request was a success or failure. These audit trails need to be administered by someone outside the security and biometrics group. That way, there can be no question as to the validity of the audit file entries.

How the employer is audited against terms of use

There is no use having a positive biometric policy if it cannot be enforced. Before the policy can be enforced, it must be seen and validated. The policy must clearly state the organization that will be responsible for the audit, the arbitrator who will be available to settle disputes, how frequently audits will happen, and how the auditor's report will be sent out.

Will biometric data be shared with third parties?

The sharing of biometric data to an unknown third party is never good. The employee loses control over his/her data and the employer may become liable for additional injuries suffered by the employee. The sharing of data must be optional, and as such, the default decision for sharing employee data must be no. To have biometric data shared requires the user to proactively opt in. Some sharing of data with law enforcement organizations may be necessary. It can be a condition of employment that all employees have background checks performed. This is a reasonable example of when data can be shared with a third party.

What options do employees have who cannot or will not use biometrics?

As much as biometrics have been hyped as the "silver bullet" to secure information technology, there will be portions of the population that will not want to, or can't, use them. For any given biometric, there is approximately 3–6% of the user population that is unable to use the biometric for one reason or another. This small group still needs strong authentication solutions offered to it. The secondary factor of authentication needs to have as much as possible the same high level of assurance as biometrics. This fallback authentication plan is what the hackers will go after. It is a lot easier to hack something that does not have biometrics as the primary means of authentication. Biometric authentication does not suffer from the same types of brute-force attacks as passwords. Fallback mechanisms should try to provide the same level of user convenience that would be enjoyed by biometrics, if possible.

Conclusion

Employers and employees both have rights and needs for privacy. While employed by a company, an employee needs to work with the employer to safeguard both parties' privacy. To assist in safeguarding this privacy, biometrics are used. The use of biometrics helps to solve many privacy issues, but the use of biometrics could potentially create new privacy concerns. To prevent biometrics from creating new privacy concerns, a positive biometric policy needs to be created. This policy needs to address the concerns and issues of the employees. At the same time, the policy needs to clearly lay out the goals that the company has in using biometric technology. Armed with the privacy information he/she may need, the employee should now feel more informed and may be less likely to fight the use of biometric technology.

In preparing a positive biometric policy statement, an employer commits to the employee to follow through on its statements. Conversely, the employee needs to be made aware of his/her responsibilities. The employee will provide authentications and moments of recognition to discharge his/her duties for the employer.

Both the employer and the employee are considered individual entities that are entering into this strong factor of authentication together. The employer will collect and manage the data, and the employee will authenticate when appropriate.

Having a positive biometric policy is not enough, however. The employer must be willing to be measured against the policy and be held accountable for shortcomings. For a biometric project to be a success, the employer needs to keep to the straight and narrow path and use biometrics only for true business reasons.

Part 2

BIOMETRIC TECHNOLOGIES

4

Biometric
Technologies

In the previous two chapters, we defined the different types of authentication and discussed the privacy concerns of using biometrics. This chapter deals directly with biometric technology. Biometric technology will be defined in terms of how the user interacts with the technology. Also, what makes a good biometric technology will be explored. Lastly, an understanding of what makes a good biometric for network access will be achieved.

User Interaction with Biometric Technology

Biometrics can be defined by the level of involvement the user needs to provide to be biometrically measured. User involvement with a biometric system falls into two categories:

1. Passive biometrics
2. Active biometrics

Passive Biometrics

A *passive biometric* does not require the user to actively submit to measurement. These types of systems are generally referred to as *covert*. They do not require the user to be aware that he/she is being biometrically measured. These systems are also seen as being invasive to the user's privacy. They are generally used in surveillance applications.

For use in a surveillance application, a database of known people must be collected and the system then watches for a matching biometric measurement. These systems are normally greatly influenced by the environment in which they are used. Passive biometrics are more suitable for use in identification systems than in authentication systems. Passive biometrics do not normally provide a single result. Normally, a set of enrolled people is returned, and a human operator makes the final match. Examples of passive biometrics are:

- Face
- Voice
- Gait

Active Biometrics

An *active biometric* requires the user to actively submit to measurement. These types of systems are generally referred to as *overt*. They require the user to be aware that he/she is being biometrically measured. These systems are seen as being supportive of the user's privacy.

Active biometrics are generally used in applications that authenticate a user's identity. They work by the user making a claim about who he/she is. The user supplies a user ID or some other unique identifier. The user then provides a biometric measurement in support of that claim. In this case, there is normally a high level of certainty attained as to the user's identity. Active biometrics are not as environmentally dependent as passive biometrics. Examples of active biometrics are:

- Fingerprint
- Hand geometry
- Retinal scanning
- Iris scanning

What Makes a Good Biometric?

A good biometric is defined in terms of:

- User acceptance
- Ease of use
- Technology costs
- Deployability
- Invasiveness of the technology
- Maturity of the technology
- Time it takes for the user to become habituated

Let's examine each of these criteria in more detail.

User Acceptance

The user acceptance of a biometric technology will decide the success of the biometric system. A user's acceptance of a biometric can be measured using quantifiable means. Quantifiable measures of acceptance are:

- Number of calls to help desk
- Number of attempted authentications
- Number of times fallback authentication mechanisms are used

Number of calls to help desk

From an initial evaluation, numerous calls to the help desk may be interpreted as a negative measurement. In actuality, a user who is making calls to the help desk may be trying to make the technology work. These users have accepted the technology and are trying to make it work, or are trying to evaluate the technology to see if it is acceptable. If the technology does not work, it is very difficult to assess its user acceptance. What we do know is that a user who calls the help desk frequently is either accepting of the technology or undecided. If the user does not support the technology, or feels that the technology is unacceptable, he/she would not call the help desk. These are the users who unplug their devices, disable the software, and never make their feelings known. These users are the hardest ones from which to get feedback. They have no vested interest in seeing the technology succeed, and thus experience no personal gain from its implementation. This type of user is difficult to quantify unless audit logs are used to look at the average number of user authentications. If a user has fewer than the average number, there is a great chance he/she is this type of user.

Number of attempted authentications

If the biometric technology being looked at has a central server or central reporting capability, the number of authentication attempts can be reported for each user. For analysis purposes, we will group users into three categories based on a population's average number of authentications for a given time period:

1. Below average
2. Average
3. Above average

Each of the above groups can be further divided into two result categories: success and failure. Let's examine each.

Below average

Before drawing conclusions from a below-average user, we need to eliminate external activities that may have reduced the user's average. The following questions need to be answered:

- Was the user away from the office during our time period?
- Is the biometric on his/her primary computing system?
- How long was the biometric installed and active on the user's computer?
- Is the user not logging out and locking his/her screens frequently?

Positive answers to the above questions could cause the collected data to be invalid and not a reliable measure of the user's acceptance of the technology. If the above questions do not explain the below-average number of authentications, then the number of failed versus successful authentications needs to be examined.

If there is a high number of successes to failures, then:

- The user may find the technology acceptable to use, but does not use his/her computer that frequently.
- The user may find the technology easy to use, but does not like using it.
- The user may not authenticate that often, but likes using the technology.

If there is a high number of failures to successes, then:

- The user may find the technology difficult to use, but is accepting of it.
- The user may not like using the technology, and this is leading to poor biometric interactions.
- The user does not accept the technology and is not trying to use the biometric properly.

In any of the above cases, the raw numbers alone are meaningless unless they are put into context. By looking at the above analysis, it could not be determined whether a user with a below-average number of authentications is accepting of the technology or not.

Average

A user with an average or near average number of authentications in a given time period is the easiest to analyze. To begin, first group the user's authentications into success and failures.

If the user is getting a higher number of successes than failures, it is very probable that the user is accepting of the technology. If the user is getting a higher number of failures than successes, it could be said that this user is accepting of the technology as well. If the user was not accepting of the technology, the user would have stopped trying to authenticate long ago. On the other hand, the user may have been undecided about the technology and trying to work with it. This user needs additional support and assistance. He/she needs to have every opportunity to decide if this is a technology he/she can accept.

Above average

A user with an above-average number of authentications for a given time period needs to have extra analysis applied. First, you should try to discover if any patterns exist in the user's audit trail. Things to look for include:

High number of sequential successes—This is the easiest pattern to recognize. It is clear that the user is having great success with the biometric and, as such, is probably very accepting of the technology. It is wise to verify that the FAR is set to a meaningful level. While a lower FAR does not mean the user is more accepting, it could hide possible disenchantment in the future. For example, at the initial stages of a project, the FAR is usually set high so that the user experiences success, and thus high acceptance. However, when the biometric system is brought into production and the FAR is decreased, user failure may increase. This sudden change in ease of use could cause the user to have a change in acceptance toward the biometric. If the biometric system being used also provides the level of FAR that the user is authenticating at and it is equal to or lower than what is used in production, it is safe to assume this user is accepting of the technology.

High number of sequential failures followed by a success—This user pattern would initially point to someone who would be less accepting of the technology due to a high number of failures per success. While this seems like a logical conclusion, other factors need to be examined. They include:

Did the user have a hard time in creating a reference template?— The most important part of biometric authentication is the enrollment process. If the user has a good enrollment and template created, future authentications are much easier. If the user in question had difficulty in enrolling, then it is possible his/her reference template is difficult to match. This could have been caused by poor placement, different enrollment position versus verification position, or poor biometric traits. If the cause is poor placement or difference in position, then a re-enrollment may solve the problem and lead to better results. If the selected biometric trait is poor (e.g., worn-out ridges on fingers), a different biometric feature (e.g., a different finger) should be used.

In this situation, if the user is still keen to use the biometric and has continued with these issues, then he/she is probably accepting of the technology.

What FAR levels does the user reach when he/she is successful?– If a user has long sequences of failures followed by a success, that can be an indication of suspicious behavior. If the successful authentication is at a very low FAR level, then the failures could be attributed to poor placement, lack of user's habituation, or the user having others try to authenticate for him/her. Any of these reasons would show that the user is accepting of the technology. Having a low FAR match means that the enrollment is good; the user has good biometric traits and can use the biometric device. It may mean that the user requires some additional remedial training.

If the successful authentication after all the failures is at a high FAR, then the user could have problems with his/her enrollment or placement, or have poor biometric traits. The resolutions for these problems were outlined earlier. It does show that the user is probably accepting of the technology. If he/she was not, the user would have complained or stopped using the technology.

Is this grouping of failures periodic or a one-time occurrence?–If there is a pattern of failures, can it be accounted for? Do the failures occur at times when the user would be returning to his/her desk, in the mornings, after lunch, or just before leaving the office? If so, then the user may just be impatient and rushing to get authenticated. If a grouping seems to occur at times that would correlate to a user's coming from a different environment, then this could be the cause of the failures. For example, if a person is coming from a very cold and dry environment into a very warm and humid environment, this could cause problems with some biometric measurements. The user needs to be instructed on how to deal with these environmental changes. Once again, if the user still uses the technology and is not complaining, then he/she is probably accepting of the technology.

If the failures seem to be a one-time occurrence, then it is more than likely they happened during the user's habituation period. During this time, the user is getting used to using the device and tends to have a higher than normal FRR. If the frequency of this grouping of failures falls off during the sampled time period, no further action is required. If it does not, then additional remedial training may be in order. In this instance, it is clear that the user is accepting of the technology.

Number of times fallback authentication methods are used

As you will read later in the book, when conducting proofs of concept, pilots, and in the deployment phase, fallback authentication methods are often provided. These fallback authentication methods allow the user to continue functioning if his/her primary means of authentication fails. In our case, the primary means of authentication is a biometric. If the user in question is often using alternative methods for authentication, then the reasons need to be analyzed before it can be stated whether the user is accepting of the technology or not. Possible reasons for using alternate authentication methods may include:

User is not suitable for using the chosen biometric—In any population, there is a fraction of the population (some say between 3% and 5% for a fingerprint biometric) that cannot use the chosen biometric. Some users do not have a physical trait that can be measured. For example, a small percentage of the population does not have fingerprints. Other times, the reason is psychological. This could include feelings of criminality, lack of trust in the technology, or religious beliefs. For others, the use of a biometric can be a challenge of dexterity. It does take a certain amount of coordination to place a finger or hand for scanning, or to position the head in front of a camera. For any of these reasons, a user may prefer using fallback methods of authentication. This is a user who would be classified as not accepting of the technology.

Lack of time and patience to become habituated—In today's world of instant gratification, having to learn a new behavior or adapting to change is often resisted. This is also the case with biometrics. No matter how simple or straightforward the use of the technology is, there will always be those who will not use it. These users will not take the time to become habituated. They believe their current methods are adequate, and do not have the time to become accustomed to a new way of doing things. These users are not accepting of the technology. They may use the technology in the future if it is mandated, but they will never accept it.

Poor instruction in use—No matter how simple and straightforward the technology appears, users will always require instructions. Some users will grasp the concepts of biometric use faster than others. Other users will require hand-holding and remedial-level instructions. A three-step approach is used to help the user fully understand the technology:

1. Formal instruction—We all learn in different ways. The first way we learn something new is from use and experimentation. We will look at something, try to figure it out, and then use it. We may become quite proficient, but there will always be gaps in our learning. Formal instruction fills in the gaps. In formal instruction, users will be shown the basic use of the technology, which most have already mastered. There will be finer points that can be gleaned from this. At some point during the training, the user will feel re-enforced by what he/she is learning, or realize that there is more to learn. Normally, this training is rushed and does not afford the user much time to absorb the information and formulate questions. This training lays the groundwork for the user to begin using the technology. If this step is missed, the user may not enjoy as great a success as would otherwise be possible. There will always be doubt that he/she is doing things correctly. This personal lack of confidence can translate into a lack of acceptance of the technology.

2. Desk visits—Nothing will garner more information from a user than showing up at his/her desk. First, the user will appreciate the time you are taking for the one-on-one visit. The user will also be more likely to ask questions that either he/she had from before, but did not feel comfortable bringing up in class, or has since formulated. Either way, being there to answer these questions directly with the user will raise the likelihood of his/her acceptance of the technology. In addition, a desk visit can also reveal how the user is interacting with the technology and uncover any potential problems that can be corrected or avoided. If the user had no follow-up after class and he/she does have issues, the user may feel that he/she is not smart enough to use the technology, and thus may not want to use it.

3. Leave-behind material—After visiting the user at his/her desk and giving one-on-one attention, leaving behind a simple, easy-to-follow pamphlet is very important. The user will feel that there is still a place to go to for answers, and the supplied number on the pamphlet will connect the user with someone who understands what a biometric is and the issues the user

may be facing. It is interesting that this section is not referred to as take-away material. Take-away material from courses is very rarely ever referenced again. A good, easy-to-read pamphlet will get used numerous times. This pamphlet can, in some ways, be the user's security blanket. This pamphlet will describe the basic use and goal of the technology. It will answer basic questions and, most importantly, it will provide the telephone number of a biometric expert. This type of reassurance for the user will greatly increase his/her acceptance of the technology.

Frequent failure of the biometric hardware–It is unfortunate when hardware fails, but it is a fact of life just like anything else. There will be bad devices in any shipment received. The percentage of these should be low if the biometric company is reputable and its product is mature. If there are continuous failures of the technology, the user will lose confidence in the system, and will be less likely to accept the technology. All biometric equipment should have gone through some sort of burn-in. During this burn-in process, electronic components have a chance to adjust to their operating environment. They will also do this through normal expansion and contraction from use. It is at this point that most failures will be found. Some hardware failures are caused by users; for example, it is known that capacitive fingerprint technology does not like electrostatic discharge. So, a user who wears lots of wool and works in a low-humidity, carpeted environment should probably ground him/herself before using such a device. Also, some biometrics that rely on camera technology do not perform well with sudden changes in contrast or very bright lights. Every effort should be made to use the devices in accordance with the vendor's operating instructions. At the same time, daily use should not cause premature failure of the device. If a user does experience frequent hardware failures, he/she will be less accepting of the technology.

Ease of Use

The success of any technology depends on its ease of use. If a technology is difficult to use, consumers will not buy it. Companies wanting to have successful products have spent considerable time and resources in this area. For biometrics, the three areas that need to be addressed in terms of ease of use are:

- Ergonomics
- FRR
- Biometric software

Ergonomics

Companies define their products' ease of use in terms of ergonomics. *Ergonomics* describe the relationship of human interaction to the use of a product. Ergonomics in biometrics place a large emphasis on ease of use. A biometric device that does not work smoothly with the human form will find itself quickly collecting dust on a shelf. The ergonomic properties that a device needs to exhibit vary from device to device and what biometric measure is being used. In general, a device must use natural human interaction to get its measure. For example, a fingerprint reader must not require the user to rotate his/her hand in such a way that is not natural. A face recognition camera must not require the user to extend his/her neck so that the face is greatly separated from the body.

FRR

Another aspect of ease of use is the FRR of the biometric system. If the biometric algorithm being used causes a high FRR, then the user will not find that system easy to use. It will require the user to make a higher number of biometric attempts to get authenticated. This will lead to user frustration and lack of acceptance.

Biometric software

Another aspect of any biometric system is the software that controls the biometric device. If the software the user needs to interface with is not easy to use, then ease of use for the user will suffer. For example, if the software that captures the biometric image does not provide some sort of feedback to the user, the user will find it more difficult to present his/her biometric. In this case, the user will be "flying blind" in presenting the biometric. Conversely, if the software provides too much feedback, or is too exacting in its requirements for acquisition, this too can decrease ease of use.

Technology Cost

No matter how easy a biometric is to use, it will never get deployed if it is too costly. The technology cost of a biometric system is made up of the following:

- Device cost
- Deployment costs
- Support

Device cost

The cost of a biometric device varies depending on the type of biometric being measured. The cost of a biometric device can also vary within the same type of biometric. Depending on the features and functionality offered, that variation in price can be upwards of 100%. A good biometric device will provide the most functionality for the cost. Any company purchasing a biometric device should examine what features are really required. For example, does your biometric application need alive-and-well detection? Does the biometric application require a trusted device? The choice of device is a tradeoff between security features and the cost of the device. If you are securing a corporate phonebook application, you will probably require a level of device different from securing the company's trade secrets.

A good device in terms of cost will meet the requirements of the application, and not break the budget for the project.

Deployment costs

Once a biometric device has been selected and the software prepared, the device and software still need to be deployed. Depending on the biometric device and software selected, desktop hardware may need to be distributed, software pushed to the desktop, and possibly, servers may need to be installed. These soft costs are often overlooked in the selection of a biometric solution. Even if the hardware itself was affordable, the cost of deploying it could be a limiting factor.

A good biometric solution will allow for a cost-effective deployment of the hardware and software.

Support

Once the hardware and software have been deployed, there is the cost of supporting the installation. If the device is prone to failure, or generates a high level of FRR, then the costs associated with supporting it will be high. The users will be calling the help desk for support. Also, if the biometric is not reliable, then the users will need to use fallback methods of authentication. These failures and costs of support will greatly decrease the expected return on investment (ROI) of the biometric solution. Cost-cutting on the hardware and software choices during the selection stage can cause greater support costs in the end.

A good biometric solution will be easy to support and allow flexibility in choice of hardware and software.

Deployability

Before a final decision is made on the hardware and software, another factor needs to be taken into account. The deployability of the solution is where the rubber meets the road. If the proposed solution is affordable, and is accepted by the users, it still may not be feasible if it is not deployable. The deployability of a solution is determined by:

- Device size
- Environmental conditions
- Infrastructure requirements
- Minimum client/server system requirements
- Deployment methodology supported by the hardware and software selection

Device size

As anyone who has walked around corporate offices will tell you, the real estate allotted per employee is dropping. This also impacts the size of the desk or office an employee has. Having to deploy a device that requires a great deal of desk or office space is not feasible. Also, the close proximity of the employees to each other can cause some biometric devices not to function optimally. For example, a hand geometry device requiring a large amount of space may not be practical to deploy on a small, crowded desktop. A voice recognition system that requires lower levels of ambient noise may not work well in a crowded trading-floor environment.

Therefore, a good biometric device is subject to the size that can be accommodated in the user's environment.

Environmental conditions

The environment in which a user works may not be conducive to certain types of biometric devices. As seen earlier, voice recognition devices do not operate well in areas with high ambient noise. Some user environments are also influenced by temperature or humidity. In too cold/hot or too humid/dry conditions, the choice of device is affected. At the same time, certain floor treatments and humidity levels may cause a great deal of static electricity to develop. In these environments, biometric devices with exposed sensors or devices not having electrostatic discharge protection may find themselves on the receiving end of over 35,000 volts from crossing a carpet with low air humidity.

The type of work being performed by the user can also generate environmental effects on a biometric device. For example, factory workers who have high grease and solvent content on their hands are not good candidates for hand-based biometrics. A clean room also poses problems for a number of biometric devices. How does one get a biometric measure from someone wearing a "bunny suit"?

A good biometric device will take into account the working environment and jobs of the end-users.

Infrastructure requirements

A biometric system can be made up of more than device and software. It can also rely on existing corporate infrastructure or require a company to implement new infrastructure. For instance, if the chosen biometric system requires backend server authentication, server hardware needs to be provided or procured. The backend data store that the biometric system will need to utilize must therefore be ascertained. Will it be an LDAP directory or a relational database? Does the company already have one or both of these in place? If not, which one will the company put into place? The need to put in new infrastructure will not only increase costs through capital expenditures, but also through ongoing support and maintenance.

A good biometric system would utilize the existing corporate infrastructure.

Minimum client/server system requirements

Most companies go through a technological refresh every three to four years. At this time, the company will acquire state-of-the-art technology to carry it through to the next technology refresh. The chosen biometric system not only needs to clearly state what its minimum system configuration is, but also what is actually usable. For example, many operating system manufacturers list minimum operating requirements. However, these minimum operating system conditions are at times barely sufficient to load the operating system. At the same time, a biometric system may list very modest requirements. Once testing is done, it may be shown with use that the biometric system works on its minimum requirements, but that it actually takes longer to authenticate. This may not be acceptable to the end-users.

A good biometric system will provide adequate performance on the previous year's state-of-the-art technology. This way, most corporations are either one year behind this minimum or are approaching a technology refresh.

Deployment methodology supported by the hardware and software selection

Once it is time to deploy a biometric system, it is unlikely that an entire corporation can be rolled out all at once. In later chapters in the book, a proper planning process is presented. For the purposes of this discussion, it is safe to say that total rollout is not achievable in a timely fashion, nor would it be prudent to attempt one. A phased or staged rollout carries the lowest risk and is the most successful. During a staged rollout, your company will be operating in three different environments. The first will be the status quo, or no biometric system in place. The second will be a hybrid of old and new. Lastly, your company will be at total rollout. The three phases can be viewed from the perspective of a company, a line of business, or a location. The choice of rolling out company-wide, by a line of business or by geographic region, should not be dictated by the technology.

A good biometric system will allow for a flexible deployment of the solution based on the methodology that is best for the company and its users.

Invasiveness of the Technology

From a user's perspective, a good biometric device will not be invasive to use. The invasiveness of a device can be viewed from the technology used to measure the biometric or the level of involvement required by the user.

The technology used to measure the biometric trait can cause invasiveness for the user. For example, a camera used to get a fingerprint is less invasive than using a camera and light to get a retina scan. Users tend to view scans of internal biometrics as more intrusive in nature than external measurements. This is normally because the technology required to scan these biometrics is more invasive.

The level of involvement of the user in the biometric system can also influence the perception of invasiveness. A biometric that a user needs to submit to can be viewed as less invasive than one that can be taken from the user. For example, finger, hand, iris, retina, and vein require the user to actively submit to the measurement. Biometrics like voice, face, and gait are seen as more invasive. This type of invasiveness is not so much concerned with the mechanics of gathering the biometric measurement, as with the loss of control over the user's biometric measures.

Thus, a good biometric would be one that is not invasive when used or when a user's biometrics are measured.

Maturity of the Technology

When selecting a biometric system, one needs to look at the time a biometric has had in the market. It is reasonable to assume that the more mature and market-tested a biometric technology is, the better it will be to use. In general, this is the case. Each successive generation of biometric technology has improved. For some, improvement has come in the methods used to measure a biometric trait, the size of a device, the cost of a device, or ergonomics. These advances are always going to happen from year to year. At what point does the buying decision occur? Does the company wait for next year's technology before purchasing? The answer depends on the application. If the biometric trait that is to be used for measurement already has a proven and reliable device, then this is the one to buy. The cost of the device may decrease if manufacturing improvements are made, but it may also increase in price if functionality is added.

When looking at the maturity of the technology for a good biometric, the buyer must remember that the technology needs to be proven, mass-produced, and not in an initial release stage.

Time It Takes for a User to Become Habituated

The ongoing success of a biometric system will depend on the user populations becoming habituated. By becoming habituated to the technology, the user's comfort level increases, as does the user's productivity. The selection of a biometric device can influence if and how quickly this habituation occurs.

Biometric systems that are ergonomic, easy to use, and mature tend to encourage the users to become habituated more quickly than ones that are uncomfortable, not easy to use and immature. Certain features of different biometric devices can aid in this. For example, a fingerprint scanner with a large surface area will allow a user to get accustomed to using it sooner than one with a smaller imaging area. A face biometric system that does not require the user to sit as still as another will allow the user to get used to it quicker.

A good biometric, then, will have features and ergonomics that will aid the user in becoming habituated.

What Makes a Good Biometric for Network Security?

A good biometric for network security would have the following characteristics:

- Users willingly accept the biometric device
- Users find it easy to use
- The total technology costs provide a suitable ROI
- The technology is deployable and supportable
- The technology is not invasive and requires the user to actively submit to its use
- The technology is mature and reliable
- Users quickly become habituated to the device

By the list of requirements above, many devices could be found. The intended use of the device, the types of users, and the location in which the users will use the device will help in narrowing down the selection.

Moving forward, in the next chapters, the different biometric technologies will be introduced. In a subsequent section, the implementation of a biometric for network security will be described.

Conclusion

There are two types of biometrics: active and passive. An active biometric device will protect and enhance the user's privacy. Beyond knowing whether or not a device is privacy-positive, it must also be discerned if it is a good biometric device by using the following quantifiable measurements:

- User acceptance
- Ease of use
- Technology costs
- Deployability
- Invasiveness of the technology

- Maturity of the technology
- Time it takes for the user to become habituated

Of all the quantifiable measurements, user acceptance requires the most analysis. The other quantifiable measures are easy to understand and define. The selection of a biometric device is determined by:

- The intended use of the device
- The types of users
- The location where the users will use the device

5

Finger Biometric Technologies

Fingerprint biometrics are the most widely used and accepted of all the biometrics. Since the fingerprint has been used as a form of identification for a long time, it has both acceptance and fear. People accept in general that fingerprints are unique and can be used to identify someone. This trust comes from governmental and law enforcement use of fingerprints. At the same time, their use of the fingerprint also causes fear about its use. Some individuals involved with fingerprint authentication for network access have expressed the feeling that using their fingerprint for authentication makes them feel like a criminal. This feeling can lead to fear of the use of fingerprint biometrics. As explained in this book, the use of biometrics must be accompanied with proper user training and communications. By doing so, biometrics can be seen as a privacy-enabling technology, not a technology to be feared. Even with the concern over the use of fingerprints, the finger biometric still remains more widely accepted than any other biometric.

Look at your fingerprints. What features do you see? Do they look crisp and clear, or wilted and smudged? Are your fingers dry or greasy? What type of work or hobbies do you do that involve your hands? The definition and quality of the finger skin can greatly influence how well a print will be imaged. The work or hobbies that one does can also influence the quality of a print. People who spend a lot of time working with their hands tend to have rougher and less-defined fingerprints. These factors can influence how well someone will be able to use fingerprint biometrics. In this chapter, we will see that some fingerprint scanning devices are better at scanning dry, less-defined fingerprints and others are better at greasy fingerprint types.

For a detailed explanation of fingerprint biometrics, the discussion will be broken down into the following areas:

- General description of fingerprints
- How is the finger imaged?
- What types of algorithms are used for fingerprint interpretation?
- How can this biometric be spoofed?

General Description of Fingerprints

The general classification of fingerprints used today came from the work of Sir Edward Henry, who published his book, *Classification and Use of Fingerprints*, in 1900. This work forms the basis for modern-day fingerprint forensics. Fingerprints are identified by both macro and micro features. The macro features of a fingerprint include:

- Ridge patterns
- Ridge pattern area
- Core point
- Delta point
- Type lines
- Ridge count

The micro features of a fingerprint are made up of minutia points. Minutia points are classified by:

- Type
- Orientation
- Spatial frequency
- Curvature
- Position

Let's examine the macro features, then the micro features of a fingerprint.

Macro Fingerprint Features

Macro fingerprint features are, as the name implies, large in size (Figure 5–1). In general, a feature is considered macro if it can be seen unaided by the human eye. The most visible macro feature seen is the ridge pattern. Others can be seen if the print has good ridge/valley definition, the lighting is good, and your eyesight is excellent!

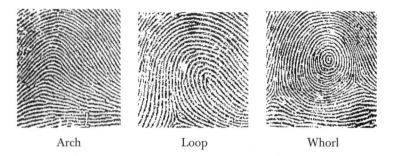

| Arch | Loop | Whorl |

Figure 5–1
Ridge patterns.

Ridge patterns

- Arch–Arches account for approximately 5% of the ridge pattern in a given population. Arches are different from loops in that arches are more open curves. Arches can also form a subgroup called tented arches. In a tented arch, the arch angle is much more obtuse than in a normal arch.
- Loop–Loops account for approximately 60% of the ridge patterns in a given population. Loops may slant left or right, or be presented as a double loop. A double loop has both a left and right loop, conforming to each other's outline.
- Whorl–Whorls account for approximately 35% of the ridge patterns in a given population. Whorls are defined by at least one ridge making a complete circle.

Ridge pattern area

The ridge pattern area is the area in the print where all the macro features are found (Figure 5–2). It is normally defined by diverging ridge flows that form a delta.

Figure 5–2
Ridge pattern area.

Core point

The core point is found at the center of the finger image (Figure 5–3). It may or may not correspond to the center of the ridge pattern area. It is used as a reference point for measuring other minutia and also during classification. Classification is the organizing of prints based on their ridge pattern.

Figure 5–3
Core point.

Delta point

"The Delta is the point on the first ridge bifurcation, abrupt ending ridge, meeting of two ridges, dot, fragmentary ridge, or any point upon a ridge at or nearest the center of divergence of two type lines, located at or directly in front of their point of divergence. It is a definite fixed point used to facilitate ridge counting and tracing."[1] In Figure 5–4, the delta point has been magnified.

Figure 5–4
Delta point.

1. J. Edgar Hoover, *Classification of Fingerprints* (Federal Bureau of Investigation, Department of Justice, U.S. Government Printing Office), 1939.

Type lines

Type lines are the two parallel innermost ridges that define the ridge pattern area. In Figure 5–5, the type lines are the two slightly darker ridge lines in the enlarged section.

Figure 5–5
Type lines.

Ridge count

Ridge count is the number of ridges that intersect a line drawn from a delta to the core. There could be more than one ridge count for each finger image. For each delta in the finger image, there will be a corresponding ridge count between it and the core. In Figure 5–6, the ridge count from the delta to the core is 12 ridges.

Figure 5–6
Ridge count.

Micro Fingerprint Features

As the name implies, micro fingerprint features cannot be seen unaided by the human eye. A number of the current fingerprint scanners on the market now have a high enough resolution that pores can be counted. What follows is a description of the minutia that make up the micro features:

- Type
- Orientation
- Spatial frequency
- Curvature
- Position

Type

There are a number of different types of minutia; the common ones are:

- Ridge ending
- Ridge bifurcation
- Ridge divergence
- Dot or island
- Enclosure or lake
- Short ridge

Ridge ending

A ridge ending is a gap in a ridge or a point where a ridge suddenly stops (Figure 5–7).

Figure 5–7
Ridge ending.

Ridge bifurcation

A ridge bifurcation occurs when a ridge splits into two or more new ridges (Figure 5–8).

Figure 5–8
Ridge bifurcation.

Ridge divergence

A ridge divergence occurs when two ridges running parallel suddenly diverge in opposite directions. In Figure 5–9, the two ridges diverge at the point where another ridge has a bifurcation.

Figure 5–9
Ridge divergence.

Dot or island

A dot or island occurs when a ridge is short enough to be perceived as a single point (dot) or straight line (island). In Figure 5–10, we can see a group of three dots or islands.

Figure 5–10
Dot or island.

Enclosure or lake

An enclosure (lake) minutia occurs when a ridge bifurcates and then rejoins itself. This then leaves a valley surrounded by the rejoined ridge. In Figure 5–11, the ridge has created two enclosures.

Figure 5–11
Enclosure or lake.

Short ridge

A short ridge is a ridge of short length, but not so short as to be considered an island or dot. In Figure 5–12, you can see two short ridges and two dots. Notice the short ridges have more of a linear look to them. The dots have more of a circular look to them.

Figure 5–12
Short ridge.

Orientation

Orientation refers to the general direction in which a minutia feature appears to be moving. In Figure 5–13, both scaled areas contain bifurcations, but their orientation is different. The bifurcation in the left-hand enlarged area would have a general slope of approximately 1. The bifurcation in the right-hand enlarged area would have a general slope of -1.

Figure 5–13
Orientation.

Spatial frequency

Spatial frequency can be viewed as the density of ridges around a given minutia point. In Figure 5–14, the spatial frequency is higher around the island at the top right than the bifurcation at the middle left.

Figure 5–14
Spatial frequency.

Curvature

Curvature is the rate of change of a ridge's direction. In the above left enlargement in Figure 5–15, the rate of change is lower, as the ridge curves are flatter. In the bottom right enlargement in Figure 5–15, the rate of change is higher, as the ridge curves are tighter.

Figure 5–15
Curvature.

Position

Position refers to the relative location of the minutia. References are normally made using a Euclidian grid, and having the origin either at the core point or at a delta. In Figure 5–16, the origin has been placed at the core point. The numbers at the end of each axis are at their maximum value. In our example, you can find a bifurcation at (1,-1) and a group of dots at (-1,1.5)

Figure 5–16
Position.

How Is the Finger Imaged?

We have seen what constitutes a fingerprint for biometric use. How the finger is imaged needs to be explained. Since fingerprint biometrics are active biometrics, the user must submit to the scan and needs to place his/her finger on the scanner for imaging. The scanning can be done with different technologies, but in general, they all need to capture an image of the finger. A fingerprint scanner captures the image and then transmits either the image or, if it is a trusted device, a secure response to the fingerprint scan. The technology used to scan fingers falls into two basic categories:

1. Optical scanners
2. Silicon scanners

Optical scanners are composed of complementary metal-oxide semiconductor (CMOS) and charge-coupled device (CCD) technology. Silicon scanners include capacitive, thermal, and radio frequency (RF). Each scanner type is discussed in more detail in the following sections.

Optical Scanners

Optical scanners use optics to gather finger images. The optics are part of a camera system that captures reflected light from a light source, normally through a prism. Regardless of whether the camera technology being used is CCD or CMOS, the basic principals for optical imaging are employed.

To get an optical fingerprint image, the device will have:

- Platen–Used for presenting the finger.
- Prism–Used for reflecting the lighted image to the camera.
- Light source–Used to illuminate the fingerprint. This is normally a grid of light-emitting diodes (LEDs).
- Camera–Used to capture the finger image.

The difference between CCD and CMOS technologies comes down to their implementation and use.

CCD is the older of the two technologies. CCD came to the market in the early 1970s. In the following decades, it has been refined and tuned to produce better and cleaner images. CCD is used for almost any digital imaging requirements. The drawbacks of CCD technology are its need for high operating voltages and the cost of additional electronics to help manage complex clocking requirements. CCD also offers only an image captured as a sequential data stream. Thus, if an imaging application wanted only one particular area of interest in an image, it would need to stream in the whole image.

CMOS is a new silicon-based imaging technology. Since the imager is based on silicon, it can be readily manufactured on any production line that is currently making silicon chips. Its ability to utilize generalized production makes CMOS a lower-cost device. Since CMOS is a solid-state component, it can also be used as the basis for systems on a chip. In this type of chip design, all the electronics for a particular task can be consolidated into a single electronic package. That is to say, a single chip could handle the tasks of imaging, processing the signal, running a USB hub, and doing encryption. This way, the total cost of the system can be lowered.

CMOS technology comes in two flavors. The first is a passive arrangement whereby the output of a row or column of pixels is detected by a single amplifier for the row, column, or entire image. Thus, to use a single amplifier, a larger capacitance is required at both the input and output amplifiers. This can increase signal noise and reduce the sensitivity of the device. This can lead to CMOS's technology having a lower resolution when compared to CCD. This is being addressed through the development of active pixel technologies. In active pixel technologies, each pixel implements its own first-stage amplifier. In doing so, the required capacitance is diminished and the signal noise is decreased. In turn, the resolution of the image is increased.

The choice of a finger biometric using either CMOS or CCD technology really comes down to questions of cost and function. If the biometric application does not have a restriction on power consumption, then CCD will be fine. On the other hand, the relatively cheap production costs of CMOS imagers will lower the price of the biometric device more rapidly. It is important to know then if the CMOS imager to be used is being implemented with passive or active pixel technologies.

Silicon Scanners

In general, silicon-based scanners require the presentation of a fingerprint directly onto a piece of silicon. As we know, silicon is a sensitive material and very susceptible to electrostatic discharge. This material provides great promise in reduced cost even with its drawbacks. This reduced cost comes from two areas. First, like a CMOS device, it can be fabricated on almost any silicon-based assembly line. Second, with the work going on to reconstruct finger images, either through swiping the finger or multiple image reconstruction of the print, smaller pieces of silicon can be used. This second point drives the cost down since the smaller the piece of silicon required to image, the higher the silicon wafer yield.

Like optical technologies, regardless of the type of imaging being used in a silicon-based scanner, the basic operations are the same. The finger is sensed in some way, and that produces an output that can be measured by the appropriate type of silicon. Thus, to get an image, the following components are common:

- Platen–Depending on the sensing technology, this may or may not be the silicon wafer itself.
- Signal generator–This generates the sensing signal that will be picked up by the silicon.
- Contact plate–The contact plate may be for electrostatic discharge or used as part of the signal generator.
- Silicon sensor–This is the silicon part of the sensor that will receive the signal reflected back from the fingerprint.

Each specific type of silicon-based sensor is described in the following sections.

Capacitive

The capacitive was the first silicon-based scanner to make it to market. Early scanners suffered from frequent failure due to electrostatic discharge. Recent improvements in the packaging and design of the devices have reduced the frequency with which this happens, but it is still an issue to be considered. Capacitive-based sensors work on a capacitance principle. That is, as the ridges of a fingerprint contact the silicon layer, a greater capacitance is created than where the valleys do not touch the silicon. The details are as follows: The silicon contains a series of capacitors packed tightly on the chip. The drive circuit for each capacitor is an inverting operational amplifier. An inverting operational amplifier works by altering its output current based on changes in the input current. Thus, to gather an image from the capacitor, the two capacitive plates are discharged and then a fixed charge is applied to each plate. As the ridges of a finger get closer and finally make contact with the chip's surface, this drives up the capacitance of that circuit. The increase in capacitance indicates the presence of a ridge. The valley of a fingerprint does not increase capacitance since there is no contact with the skin. Thus, all the drive circuits are queried and a finger image is created for comparison.

Thermal

A thermal fingerprint sensor does not rely on generating a signal externally. Thermal sensors use the body's own heat as the signal to measure. As a finger contacts the surface of the sensor, the ridges and valleys provide a temperature difference. The temperature difference is measured between the nominal temperature of the sensor before the finger is presented and after. The difference generates a signal through a pyro-electric effect. The time required to measure the delta in temperature between the nominal temperature and the measured temperature is in microseconds. This allows for quick fingerprint imaging. As such, this makes this type of sensor ideal for a swipe form factor. In a swipe form factor, the finger is swiped across a thin piece of silicon and the finger image is reconstructed from distinct captured frames. Since the swipe form factor is very small, the cost of the silicon for the sensor is lower because more sensors can be taken from one wafer of silicon.

Radio frequency (RF)

An RF fingerprint sensor works by imaging the live layer below the skin. To accomplish this, the sensor uses two parallel plates that generate an electric field between them. As a finger comes into contact with an exposed drive plate, the finger causes the signal to attenuate, and this attenuation is captured by the sensors in the silicon below. The ridges on the finger cause the signal to attenuate more than the valleys. This type of sensor works very well for dry and calloused fingers. It also works relatively well with non-conductive coatings on the fingers.

Types of Algorithms Used for Interpretation

Now that we know what constitutes a fingerprint and how it can be imaged, we need to know which types of algorithms are used. The algorithms used to match and enroll fingerprints fall under the following categories:

- Minutia-based
- Pattern-based
- Hybrid algorithm

Minutia-Based Algorithm

Earlier in this chapter, the minutia of fingerprints were described. As such, vendors who choose to use minutia-based algorithms will need to provide the highest-quality image possible. This way, the most minutia will be preserved. In addition, the presentation of the fingerprint after templating need not be as exact. The minutia in the template are compared to the raw template and matches are made. Minutia-based templates are relatively smaller than pattern-based matching templates.

This type of algorithm would be good to use in a situation where template sizing is important. For example, doing a match on a card would be more efficient with a minutia-based algorithm. For minutia-based fingerprint algorithms, only a small part of the finger image is required for verification. As such, it is ideal to have as much minutia as possible in the finger imaging area. Since just a portion of the minutia is required for verification, it would be ideal to use this algorithm where space restrictions impact the use and deployment of biometrics. Thus, a good imager for a minutia-based algorithm would be one that takes a high-quality image and has a large enough capture window for the relative core of the fingers to be imaged and captured.

Pattern-Based Algorithm

Pattern-based matching algorithms use both the micro and macro features of a fingerprint. When the macro features are utilized, the size of the image required for authentication, when compared to the size of the image needed for minutia-only requirements, is larger. Since only the macro features need to be compared, these types of algorithms tend to be fast and have a larger template size. They also require more of the image area to be present during verification. A good imager for pattern-based matching algorithms is one that has a high-quality camera and a large enough scanning surface to capture the important macro details.

Hybrid Algorithm

As the name implies, a hybrid algorithm uses the best features from the minutia-based algorithms and those from pattern-based matching. This algorithm is a good all-purpose algorithm, giving a good tradeoff between the accuracy of the minutia algorithm and the speed of pattern-based recognition. This algorithm would require the resulting template to be slightly larger than a minutia template, and smaller than a pattern-based matching algorithm. A high-quality optical sensor is best for this type of algorithm. It would offer a large enough image area, with very good quality for the images. The hybrid algorithm takes longer to enroll because of the use of both minutia and pattern-based recognition. Once this has occurred, the matching is actually faster than the minutia-based algorithm.

Which Algorithm Is Best?

This question can be answered positively for any algorithm given the right environment. With the right conditions, the pattern-based algorithm and minutia-based algorithm perform equally well. More important are the generalized cases for which a finger biometric may be used.

To decide on an algorithm, the use and implementation of the biometric need to be examined. If

- Template size is not important
- The relative speed differences between minutia-based and pattern-based algorithms are negligible
- The application does not require high throughput

then a pattern-based algorithm would work best. Otherwise, if

- Template size is important
- The relative speed difference is sufficiently meaningful given the volume of transactions
- The application has a high throughput

then a minutia-based algorithm will work best. Otherwise, if

- Template size is not important
- Faster matching is required than enrollment
- The application has high throughput

then a hybrid algorithm will work best.

How Can this Biometric be Spoofed?

The risk of using any new technology needs to be evaluated. The risks to a company using a biometric device are an improvement over just the simple password used today. The risk model used needs to be one of balance. That is, one should bear in mind the tradeoff between increased security and decreased user convenience, and consider the converse as well. If you decrease security, user convenience will increase. This password paradox can be negated by the fact that a biometric device will provide increased user convenience as a result of being able to use something the user has. As a consequence, the user no longer needs to remember his/her network password. Since that password is replaced by something the user always has or the password is proxied on the user's behalf, this in essence increases the security of the system.

Attacks on a finger biometric system fall into the following categories:

- Attacking the physical finger
- Using artifacts
- Attacking the communications
- Compromising the template
- Attacking the fallback system

For each type of attack, a recourse is offered.

Attacking the Physical Finger

This is the type of attack that gets the most press. We have all seen this in the movies, where the hero or villain fakes someone's fingerprints. This is normally done through the lifting of a latent print or, if the movie is more edgy, the removal of the finger itself.

Until recently, it was believed that the biggest threat in this area came from the compromise of a user's print through the user's own complicity. It was felt that to get a sufficiently detailed "fake finger," the user having his/her finger faked needed to be present and complicit. That is, he/she would need to voluntarily offer a finger for faking. This could be done through a malleable material that would conform and stick to the conspirator's finger. Thus, this attack was generally categorized in the same way as the sharing of passwords.

This view on the making of fake fingers from willing accomplishes changed on January 24, 2002. At the conference for The International Society of Optical Engineering (SPIE), Tsutomu Matsumoto et al. presented a paper showing not only the creation of a fake finger from a willing participant, but also the possible clandestine duplication from a lifted print.

While the procedure used by Tsutomu to make a fake finger from a willing participant was very similar to the classic technique described above, he introduced a new element for producing a fake finger from a latent print.

For the creation of a fake finger from a lifted print, Tsutomu needed a high-quality latent image. In his experiment, he retrieved his print from a flat sheet of glass that a full impression was left on. The sheet of glass was then fumed using a cyanoacrylate compound. Cyanoacrylate is better known to the rest of us as the active adhesive agent found in glues and, if applied to the skin, will cause the skin to stick to itself. The fact that cyanoacrylate will cause skin to adhere to just about anything makes it ideal for finding and imaging latent prints. A residual fingerprint is initially made up of water and other biological compounds. As the water evaporates, the print that is left behind is composed of amino acids, glucose, lactic acid, and other sundry biological agents. What cyanoacrylate fuming does is bond the molecules of cyanoacrylate to the residual biological agents. This new enhanced print is now easier to handle and image.

To get a very clear image of the print, Tsutomu used a high-end microscope to image the print, and then enhanced it using image software. Once the print was digitized and enhanced, he then printed it onto a transparency. Once the print was on a transparency, he then cut out the print and applied the transparency with the print on it as a mask for an ultraviolet- (UV-) etchable Printed Circuit Board (PCB). Once the board was exposed to UV light with the fingerprint mask attached, the PCB board was left with an image of the finger, with the ridges and valleys inverted. That is, where there should have been a ridge, there was a valley, and where there should have been a valley, there was a ridge. Once the gummy mixture was sufficiently soft, it was applied to the PCB and a proper fingerprint shape was created. When Tsutomu had his finger, he was then able to fool a number of capacitance and optical scanners. It is interesting to note that he did not try an RF-based scanner. It is my hypothesis that the RF scanner would have been unable to image since there was no underlying ridge and valley structure to reflect the waves that would penetrate the gummy finger.

Mitigating this attack

While it is clear from the example that Tsutomu showed great ingenuity in creating a new type of fake finger that could fool a number of sensors, it also proves the adage that given enough time, money, and energy, any system can be defeated. What the adage does not tell us is what we need to interpret. That is, how easy in the real world would it be to accomplish this? Consider the following:

- Most latent prints are partial—When you leave a latent print behind, it is normally smudged or incomplete. Just ask any forensic team member at your local police department. This partial print will make it harder to get a workable fake. The partial that is left behind may not be the parts of the fingerprint enrolled in the template.
- Most surfaces that could be used for latent prints are not that easy to work with—If you look at the items that you spend most of

your time touching or using in a day, they are generally covered in plastic, and as such, not the easiest things to get latent prints from. Very rarely in a day do we touch a flat piece of glass in such a way as to leave a full print. One such flat piece of glass could be a computer monitor. Routinely, we touch a monitor when referencing an item on the screen or demonstrating to a colleague. If a monitor was used as the source of a latent image, we would probably notice either the fume hood over the monitor or the cyanoacrylate print on the screen. It should be noted that cyanoacrylate fuming is a destructive methodology that leaves the latent print permanently affixed to the host of the print.

- The use of cyanoacrylate is not exactly a "rinse-lather-repeat" procedure–If the host item containing the latent print is fumed too little or too much, the print either becomes under-developed or over-developed. Secondly, once visual through cyanoacrylate fuming, latent images need to be digitized with a high-resolution device. While digital photography continues its advance on resolution, it will be awhile before it can match the resolution and power of the microscope used by Tsutomu. This is not an item you will find at a local high school. Common items that one would have around the office do not work well either. In my own experiments, CD jewel cases, telephones, keyboards, and most mice provided poor surfaces for imaging.

- Use a sensor with "alive-and-well" detection–Alive-and-well detection refers to a device's ability to determine if the presented finger is alive and well. Techniques used have included pulse detection, temperature, capacitance, and blood oxygen level. Of all the countermeasures listed above, Tsutomu would probably be able to defeat pulse by squeezing the gummy finger, temperature by sufficiently heating the gummy finger, and capacitance either by blowing on the sensor or lightly dampening the fake finger. The hardest one to fake would be blood oxygen. Since the sensor measures the dilution of oxygen in the blood in the finger, there would need to be an introduction of a liquid that could make this happen. Additionally, all the countermeasures rely on physiological traits that can vary widely from one individual to another. The tolerances on any of these countermeasures could be so loose as to make them meaningless The only reason for implementing them in a scanner would be to increase the time, money, and effort that an attacker would need to expend to defeat the system. There is also a money tradeoff for the user of the scanner. Implementing these countermeasures would increase the cost of the unit. When deploying 10,000 devices, additional cost increases are less tolerated.

- Random finger authentication—In this countermeasure, the user of the system would register up to 10 multiple fingers. When the user came to authenticate, he/she would be challenged to present the proper finger. This would pose an issue for an attacker using a fake finger, as the attacker would need to know what finger the lifted print matches. In addition, the system could also prompt for a sequence of fingerprints.
- Use multi-factor authentication—Biometrics used in conjunction with a token for authentication would make any fake finger meaningless without the token. Now, not only does the attacker have to get your prints and know what fingers they are from, but he/she also needs your token. The time and effort to mount a successful attack have just increased since another factor of authentication would also need to be compromised.

As you can see, this attack is novel and has raised the bar in terms of creativity. It is also clear that the general fear, uncertainty, and doubt (FUD) around this vulnerability was truly a tempest in a teapot. The use of additional factors of authentication, alive-and-well detection, or finger challenge and response can adequately deal with this threat.

Using Artifacts

As we saw in the attack on the physical finger, the latent prints or artifacts we leave behind can be exploited. This particular attack focuses on artifacts left on the scanning device itself. It is only logical to assume that if we touch a device, we will leave some trace of us behind. This trace could then be exploited in some way to trick the biometric system into authenticating us. For this to work, the sensor would need to be fooled into thinking a new finger placement has taken place and image the artifact. From the previous discussions on the types of imagers used, we know that RF devices require an image of the live skin below the external layer of skin on the finger. Therefore, it is very unlikely that artifacts can be used on an RF scanner. For optical and capacitance devices, it may be possible.

Artifact use on capacitance scanners normally involves tricking the scanner into thinking a finger is present. The sensor images are based on a sufficient change in capacitance. This change in capacitance is normally accomplished in the finger through its moisture content. To duplicate this with an artifact, an attacker could breathe or blow across the surface of the imager, or use a thin-walled plastic bag with water in it laid on the imager.

For an optical device to be tricked into using an artifact, it needs to have a frame snapped by the camera. Most optical systems detect the presence of a fingerprint from a change in luminance. This can be accomplished by shining bright lights into the camera system, or by covering the platen with a hand, darkening it sufficiently to simulate a finger placement.

Mitigating this attack

What is clear from the outline of this attack is that just the presence of an artifact allows the attacker to attempt an attack. Secondly, the attacker is generally not changing the latent print. To mitigate such an attack, the following could be done:

- Remove the artifact–There are a number of ways to accomplish this. The first is through software. The firmware of a device could remember the last finger imaged. If the next finger imaged is a very close or exact match, it can discard that image. This works since the human placement of a finger on a scanner has sufficient entropy to prevent an exact placement as the last time. Additionally, the imager could use a swipe-style image placement. That is, for a finger to be imaged, it is dragged across the platen. This has the effect of erasing the print as it is read. Also, the artifact could be removed through some mechanical means such as a door closure on the platen or some other wiping mechanisms.
- Use alive-and-well detection, as previously described.
- Require that the biometric system not accept the same print twice in a row–By having more than one print enrolled, the biometric system could force the user to authenticate with a print different from the one used before. This way, the latent image becomes useless, as it would be from the previous attempt.

Like physical finger attacks, artifact attacks can be easily mitigated.

Attacking the Communication Channels

If an attacker cannot compromise a system at the point of collection, the next logical spot to compromise is the communication path. If the information being transmitted could be changed so that a false positive or a false rejection occurs, the attacker has succeeded. To do this, the attacker may physically tap the line between the device and the PC. He/she could install software on the PC (Trojan software) to intercept the template before local or remote comparison. Lastly, the attacker may try to replay a previously successful authentication attempt.

Mitigating this attack

While the general principles of securing a biometric transaction are covered later in this book, for our purposes here, the following will mitigate the above risks:

- Real-time line monitoring—With the advent of USB, it is now possible for a device or host to monitor the quality of any connection between the host and a peripheral. This includes voltage and lost packets. If the voltage drops unexpectedly or the lost packets increase in number, this could signal to the host or peripheral that the physical communication link has been compromised.
- Trojan software—If there was Trojan software on the host, many security products could possibly detect the Trojan and alert the user. The biometric system on the host could implement a secure memory model. In a secure memory model, named pipes are used and, when memory is transferred between processes, it is done using a Diffie-Hellman key exchange with a station-to-station protocol. The biometric system could also be implemented as a trusted device. See Chapter 11 for more details.
- Prevent replay attacks—Like preventing an artifact attack, biometric software could reject an exact image playback. It could also sign each frame so that the timestamp could be verified. If the timestamp was from the past, the template could be discarded. The device and host could set up session keys that would keep transactions aligned and not allow any out-of-sequence transaction to be used.

The prevention of replay attacks can be accomplished through the application of some programming fundamentals and by using standard encryption schemes.

Compromising the Template

Moving up the attack food chain, if the capture and communications of the comparison template prove to be impossible, then a compromise of the stored reference template might be attempted.

To modify the reference template, an attacker could attack the medium on which the template is stored, the machine providing the template, or the template itself while in transit to the comparison host.

Mitigating this attack

This attack is very similar to attacking the communications. To guard against this type of attack, some simple network security procedures can help:

- Protect the storage medium–Where the reference template is stored is just as important as how the template was protected in its trip for storage. Whether the template is stored in an LDAP directory, a normalized database, or a proprietary format database, proper security precautions should be taken. This includes patching the storage location with the latest releases and making sure passwords are set, strong, frequently changed, and are not the default value.

- Protect the storage host–The medium on which the template is stored needs to be protected as well. This includes patching the storage location with the latest releases and making sure passwords are set, strong, frequently changed, and are not the default value. Also, unnecessary services and other input/output (I/O) should be stopped and discouraged. Additional services or programs running on a machine may provide an entry point for an intruder to exploit. Also, physical access to the machine itself should be restricted. If a machine can be reached physically, it can be compromised.

- Protect the template in transit–Like preventing a replay attack, the information being communicated between the storage medium and comparison host needs protection. This could involve using secure socket layers (SSL) or other secure protocols, encrypting, and signing the contents.

Once again, some simple networking and security common sense can provide adequate protection against this type of attack.

Attacking the Fallback System

In any biometric system, there will never be 100% coverage of the user base. Additionally, some users will have biometric failings from time to time that will require them to use a different factor of authentication. These fallback systems are also open to attack. If the strongest point of a system is the biometric aspect, then an attacker will focus on the weaker parts. In general, this is the fallback system.

Mitigating this attack

Because this type of attack is very fluid and changes from biometric system to system, the best policy to adopt is to make the fallback as strong as possible. If the fallback for your users is a user ID and password, then make the password sufficiently strong to prevent easy password attacks. Also, if the user falling back is normally using biometrics, then make his/her password expire within a short period of time. That way, the chances of a successful compromise are lower. If possible, assign a token and password for fallback so that the attacker would need both of them for a fallback attack.

Conclusion

Fingerprint biometrics provide a very robust and mature choice for a biometric technology. As such, there are many solutions on the market. The choices within the marketplace allow a company to pick the solution that is most right. With this maturity also comes familiarity. This familiarity has allowed attackers to study and try different types of attacks on fingerprint readers. A company therefore needs to evaluate its risk structure and find the right tradeoff between user convenience and security. The security part of the tradeoff involves analyzing the level of effort needed to compromise the system and the possible loss of data or time.

6

Face Biometric Technologies

Face biometrics are used by everyone every day. The face is the first defining characteristic that we use to identify someone. It is the face that is recalled when trying to remember what someone looks like. We use it, and eventually come to depend on it, for recognition. We carry photo IDs that we show as proofs of identity. On the cards are pictures of our face.

Our trust in our ability to judge if we know someone by his/her face can also fool us as well. We have all at one time or another thought we recognized someone's face, only to have it not be the person we thought. For many people, including parents, twins present a unique problem. Some twins can be so similar that even the parents may need to identify them by some other means. The human brain is complex and, some would argue, the most powerful computer in the world. It has specialized functions for senses, but even it can be fooled. Not surprisingly, the use of face biometrics for identification is often questioned. Can it deliver the same level of accuracy as other biometrics, and can it be deployed for use in a network security environment?

In our investigation of face biometrics, we will try to answer these questions and provide a suitable background so that you can make the final decision.

To learn the most about face biometrics, the discussion will be broken into the following areas:

- General description of face biometrics
- How is the face imaged?

- What types of algorithms are used for facial interpretation?
- How can this biometric be spoofed?

General Description of Face Biometrics

The face is made up of many distinct micro and macro elements. The macro elements include the mouth, nose, eyes, cheekbones, chin, lips, forehead, and ears. The micro features include the distances between the macro features, or a reference feature and the size of the feature itself. Also, unseen to the human eye is the fact that our bodies and faces radiate heat, which can be measured by using infrared cameras. All these features can be used by face biometric systems to help identify and authenticate someone. The use of these traits is described in greater detail in the section regarding algorithms.

How Is the Face Imaged?

Facial images can be captured either through a live scan or through the use of photographs or video. Some algorithms will not support the use of a photograph or video image, as depth and other types of measurements are required. If a photograph is imaged, then a high-quality scanner is used and the photo is processed into a facial template. While infrared cameras are used for facial imaging, they are not considered here since they are not suitable for use as network security biometric devices. Their price point and size make them currently impractical to use and deploy.

Cameras that are currently usable for network security access are generally the same ones used for desktop video conferencing. They are low in cost since they use popular CCD and CMOS image technologies. They are also small enough to be deployed on a desktop. Also, they do not require any special imaging boards and they support standard connections like USB.

What Types of Algorithms Are Used for Facial Interpretation?

Now that we know what constitutes a facial image and how a face can be imaged, we need to know what types of algorithms are used. The algorithms used to match and enroll a face fall into the following categories:

- Eigenface
- Local feature analysis
- Neural network
- Automatic face processing

Eigenface

Eigenface is based on a patented technology from MIT. Eigenface, loosely translated, means "one's own face." The algorithm works from two-dimensional grayscale images. From a grayscale image, an Eigenface is extracted. The face is then mapped to a series of Eigenvectors, which are mathematical properties describing the unique geometry of that particular face, forming the biometric template. The template is then compared to the generated Eigenfaces for comparison. The degree of variance between the template and the reference Eigenfaces determines a match. The lower the variance between the template and the reference Eigenfaces, the greater the likelihood of a match (Figure 6–1).

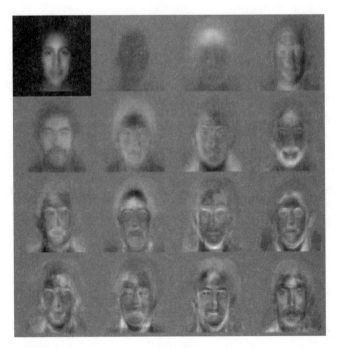

Figure 6–1
Standard Eigenfaces. (Source: MIT Media Lab, www-white.media.mit.edu.

The Eigenface algorithm is somewhat unique when doing one-to-many match identification. To create the reference template that the live template is compared to, it builds a composite of all enrolled faces. This means that as more faces are added to the database, the reference template is updated. Most Eigenface-based systems with 100–150 facial images create a reference template that can be used for comparison.[1]

Local Feature Analysis

Local feature analysis was developed by Dr. Joseph Atick, Dr. Paul Griffin, and Dr. Norman Redlich of the Visionics Corporation. Local feature analysis uses the macro features of the face as reference points.

The algorithm first locates the face from its surroundings. The reference points are then located by using the change in shading around each feature. Once a change in shade is found, it is defined as an anchor point. Once all the anchor points are found, the algorithm creates triangles that tie together the anchor points. The angles of the triangles from each anchor point are measured and a 672-bit template is generated. If there is a change in lighting intensity or orientation, this could cause the shading on the face to change. This change in shading would lead to the creation of a different template.

When a live facial scan is done, a new template is created using local feature analysis; this new template is compared against the reference templates. The higher the percentage of the comparison, the greater the likelihood that the live template and the reference template will match.

Figure 6–2 shows a face to which local feature analysis has been applied. First, the face is distinguished from the background, then local feature analysis is performed. The last image shows a scaled-up image of local feature analysis (the difference in shading is apparent).

Neural Network

The neural network algorithm is patterned after the synapses and neurons in the human brain. By creating an artificial neural network (ANN), problems can be solved based on training the network. To train the network, a series of captured faces are fed into the network. Each face has its macro features identified. In addition to having faces with

---

1. J. Velasco, "Teaching a computer to recognize a friendly face," *The New York Times*, Oct. 15, 1998, p. G7.

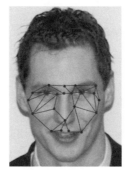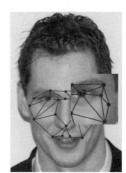

Figure 6–2
Application of local feature analysis.

identified features, other random images are added to the training set. The random images added to the training set cause the ANN to learn what does not constitute a face. Then, as the ANN begins to learn, faces are entered into the system that do not have their macro features identified. The unidentified faces that fail to match are re-entered into the system with identified features.

The ANN is made up of the following parts:

- Face detection and framing
- ANN input level
- Receptive fields
- Hidden units
- Output

Each part of a basic ANN is discussed below.

Face detection and framing

As a face is imaged, it needs to be separated from its background. Once the face is isolated from the background, it is framed and transformed to the appropriate size. It is then ready for the ANN input level.

ANN input level

Once the face is the appropriate size, the face image is put into the ANN input level. At this point, the face image is converted into pixels to meet the size specifications of the ANN input. If the input buffer is 20 pixels by 20 pixels, and the image is the same size, then each pixel maps directly to an input neuron.

Receptive fields

When the image is translated into the neurons that make up the input level, the input neurons are mapped to receptive fields. The mapping of the receptive fields is normally chosen to reflect the general characteristics of the face. For example, receptive neurons may be grouped so that the input neurons can be equally divided into squares and mapped to a single neuron. This would be a large square area for mapping where general face features can be isolated. From here, additional receptive neurons may take varying degrees and shapes of input neurons to help isolate macro features like the nose, eyes, mouth, and ears.

Hidden units

Hidden units have a one-to-one neuron/receptive field relationship. This way, a hidden unit can determine if the appropriate feature was located.

Output

The resulting output from the hidden units comes down to a single output neuron. Based on a previously chosen threshold, an output neuron may indicate a positive face match or a negative face match.

Now that we know how an ANN works, it can be applied to the problem of authentication and identification. To apply an ANN to authentication, a series of training faces are taken and then compared to a live template that is a true match. The ANN is given a chance to match the face and, if it fails, the ANN is adjusted so that a match is found. Figure 6–3 shows a generalized ANN for face processing.

Automatic Face Processing

Automatic face processing is the simplest of all the facial recognition algorithms. This algorithm works on the basis of measuring the size of a macro feature and the distances between the macro features of the face. The resulting ratios that can be created are used to form the facial template. Once the ratios are calculated, the templates are binned based on different primary ratios. For example, faces may be binned based on the distance between the eyes, or the width of the mouth.

Which Algorithm Is Best?

Face biometrics and their use can be greatly influenced by the conditions in which they are used. The focus of our work here is using biomet-

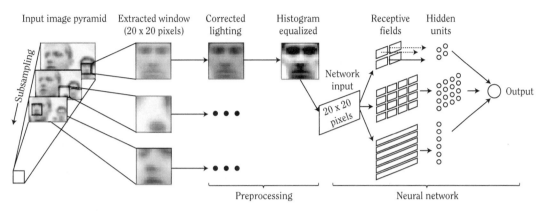

Figure 6–3
Generalized ANN for face processing. (Source: Asim Shankar and Priyendra Singh Deshwal, "Face Detection in images:Neueral Networks & Support Vector Machines," Indian Institute of Technology, Kanpur, April 2002, p. 7.)

rics for network access. As such, this biometric would be used mainly in offices with generally acceptable lighting conditions. The user would normally be seated at his/her desk for verification and would generally be authenticating based on a claim of identity. This claim of identity could take the form of inserting a smart card or providing a user ID. In addition, the user would authenticate at least three to four times a day. The speed of the authentication would need to be sufficient to make it usable, and it is quite possible that the facial expression would not always be the same. With these as our parameters, each algorithm is evaluated as to its suitability for this environment.

Eigenface

The Eigenface algorithm is relatively quick with its searches. It generally requires good lighting and the face to be presented in a full frontal orientation. Both of these can be accommodated within our parameters. It does not deal well with variations in facial expression. As such, the user would need to present a face that is always non-expressive. This may not always be possible. Additionally, it is not consistent with people who sometimes wear glasses or grow beards. This may require the user to be re-enrolled if the user wears glasses all the time has a beard.

Eigenface is a good general-purpose algorithm to use when the user community is relatively controlled and conditioned. It may not be appropriate for less structured user communities. The fact that wearing glasses and beard growth affects the algorithm's ability to authenticate could lead to a large FRR. This in turn could lead to more calls to the help desk and reduced user satisfaction.

Local feature analysis

Local feature analysis uses macro facial features along with bone structure and changes in shading to define anchor points. As such, it is much more forgiving for less than ideal lighting conditions and users who sometimes wear glasses and grow beards. The facial expression is not as critical because the bone structure does not change based on expression. It can also tolerate the face not being presented in a full frontal view. Since the macro features and bone structure are used as the anchor points, the head does not have to be held still for imaging to occur.

In general, local feature analysis is very suitable to use as a network security biometric.

Neural network

Neural network uses a learning method to teach the network how to recognize and differentiate the face. As such, it is very good at isolating the face from a complex background. While some office areas may seem more "jungle-like" than others, in general, office environments are relatively uncluttered. The algorithm also requires a large database of images to get bootstrapped, and therefore, can be slower in processing the requested face for authentication. Additionally, the neural network requires a full frontal view of the face with good lighting. This requirement is within our parameters of the office environment.

While the neural network does a good job of face recognition in complex environments, the office world does not require this level of sophistication. Therefore, the tradeoffs in using the algorithm in an office setting with controlled conditions are not sufficient to make it suitable for biometric network access.

Automatic face processing

Automatic face processing is a very quick and efficient algorithm. Its use of macro feature measurements and sizing, combined with binning, makes it a winner in lookup speed. What is known is that variation in facial expression will affect its measurements on items like mouth width and distance to other macro features. Other measurements may also be affected by changes in expression. It does work well in dimly lit areas.

This is not a requirement for our needs because office environments are generally well-lit. In addition, there could be a relatively large FAR for this algorithm. There is the question of sufficient entropy in the human face to make the metrics meaningful enough for use. In a one-to-one match, the FAR may be sufficiently low enough to make it useful. Where this algorithm may be useful is for convenience when the possibility of a false acceptance is acceptable for the tradeoff of having a much lower FRR.

Recommended facial algorithm

It appears from our analysis of facial algorithms that local feature analysis is the most suitable for biometric network access. What is being compared here is the state-of-the-art at this time. There are constant improvements being made to all the above-mentioned algorithms. For you to make the most informed decision on what algorithm to use, review what the use environment will be like, and what the goal of the system is. From here, a list of general assumptions can be compiled to select a group of vendors that may provide the most applicable algorithms and devices. Once this is done, the methodology described for conducting a proof of concept, then a pilot, and eventually a deployment will help you make a final decision.

How Can This Biometric Be Spoofed?[2]

As discussed in the opening of this chapter, even humans can be fooled into thinking they recognize a face when they do not. If this is the case, it is believable and predictable that a face biometric system could be fooled as well. While it is generally accepted that face biometrics do not provide the same level of FAR as other biometrics, face biometrics offer other very attractive attributes. It is accepted by most people that we readily use our face for recognition every day. As such, face biometrics are widely accepted. Face biometrics can also operate with a relatively low-cost imaging device. These positive qualities make face biometrics attractive.

Face biometrics are like any other biometric: susceptible to some level of spoofing. What follows is a discussion of face biometric spoofing.

---

2. This section is based on the work from C'T (*www.heise.de/ct/english/02/11/114/*), Nov. 2002, p. 114.

Attacks on a face biometric system fall into the following categories:

- Attacking the physical face
- Using artifacts
- Attacking communications (see Chapter 5)
- Compromising the template (see Chapter 5)
- Attacking the fallback system (see Chapter 5)

Attacking the Physical Face

Face biometrics are passive. That is, a biometric sample can be taken from you without your knowledge or consent. Just think of the number of pictures of you that you know about. The number of pictures you know about is likely quite high. While the majority were probably taken with your knowledge, with you posing for the picture, others were taken without your realizing it. What about pictures in which you just appear in the background? What about the picture taken by the surveillance camera at your bank? What about the camera at the tollbooth for catching drivers who run the toll? Now, imagine that someone wanted to get your picture. How hard would it be? All that person needs to do is wait for you outside your house, place of work, favorite restaurant, or a shopping center. There is no real way to know for sure that your image has not been captured. It is this very thing that makes the face biometric ripe for spoofing.

Once a facial image is captured, how it is spoofed to the system is dependent on what facial characteristics are required to acquire the image. What follows are some of the methods by which a clandestinely acquired face can be presented:

- A two-dimensional image–This is normally a photograph or an enlargement that is presented to a facial scanner. This method generally works for systems that do not use active eye recognition or depth perception for face acquisition. Active eye recognition uses the reflective nature of the pupil to identify the location of the eyes and, in turn, the other macro facial features. Depth perception is normally accomplished through the adjusting of the camera's focal length to focus on macro features that are at different depths. Though this is in general a good method, it can be fooled by moving the facial image closer and farther away from the camera until the image is captured.
- A two-dimensional image with eye cutouts–This is good for scanners that require the acquisition of the face from the pupil

location. The spoofer takes the victim's face and cuts out the pupil area for the pupils to show through. The image and face behind are presented to the scanner until an image is captured. This type of attack can be mitigated to a certain degree by the requirement of the face to show movement. This would be hard to duplicate with a two-dimensional, flat image.

- Replay of captured video—This is generally done through the clandestine gathering of video footage showing the face of the intended victim. The video is then edited and enhanced to show the victim's facial features and associated movement. This can also be done through the use of a series of stills played back in a looping video stream. This works since most facial capture devices rely on individual frames for detection, when processing a video stream. This is done to reduce the needs for increased processing and possibly specialized hardware. The video can be played back to the camera on some small video screen, like a laptop or handheld DVD player. With the advent of higher-definition video data recorders, this type of attack becomes more practical because of the increase in video quality and the reduced cost of such devices.

Mitigating this attack

While not every attack is foolproof, many are very close to always compromising the system. As pointed out above, some of the attempted compromises have relatively easy countermeasures. Once a countermeasure is introduced, the spoofer can take it to the next level. What is required to defeat this type of spoofing is a holistic approach, which uses the best of all the anti-spoofing techniques.

In the above attacks, the spoofed image could be either moved or imaged in such a way to make it fool the system. What all the spoofing methods had in common was that the spoofed image needed to be recorded. That is, it needed to be a static presentation. Whether those static presentations took the form of a two-dimensional image or a loop of video, taken as a whole, they were all static.

What is needed to trick the spoofer is a dynamic measure of the face. Some have suggested using actions such as the blinking of the eyes or the movement of the face with breathing. These are all good starts, but with a little thought and ingenuity, these could be compensated for. What is really required is an indeterminate challenge and response method. The challenge and response method used would depend on the algorithm's ability to utilize a facial feature for recognition. Thus, the user could be asked to blink his/her eyes a certain number of times, or in a particular pattern. The user could be asked to turn his/her head in a particular direction, or change the shape of the mouth. These types of challenge and response methods would require the spoofer to create a spoofed model of the victim with such a high level of detail that it becomes prohibitively expensive or complex.

Using Artifacts

Since face biometrics are passive and do not require the user to actively submit to measurement, there is no physical contact between the user and the scanner. This means that the artifacts left by facial scanning are different from the type left by fingerprints. Facial artifacts are normally in the form of image files that were used by the system during capture. As such, they could provide a wealth of knowledge and data for replay attacks against a biometric system. It should be sufficient with proper programming not to leave these types of files behind. Even if they are erased, they can be recovered and then their contents could be used unless they are overwritten.

Mitigating this attack

To mitigate this attack, do not use a physical file for the video stream or, if needed, encrypt it using (ideally) PKI. This way, only the process can read the contents and the secret used for encrypting is not shared or embedded in the application itself.

Conclusion

Face biometrics present a very attractive system to use for network access. As we saw, local feature analysis provided the most suitable algorithm for use based on certain assumptions. However, there are some tradeoffs in its use. Namely, the user is required to be presented in good light and to hold still as much as possible. Also, because face biometrics being passive, there can be concerns over spoofing and privacy. Consequently, a company needs to evaluate its risk structure and find the right tradeoff between user convenience, cost, and security. The security part of the tradeoff involves analyzing the level of effort required to compromise the system, and the possible loss of data or time.

7

Voice Biometric Technologies

The use of voice for biometric authentication seems natural and appropriate. From an early age, we learn to recognize the sound of our parents' voices. Voice provides a very important source of sound for the sense of hearing. The interpretation of a voice we perceive can tell us a lot about someone. It can tell us their relative distance to us, their emotion, and, most importantly, we can associate the voice with someone we know. Like recognizing a face, we have all made the mistake of thinking that we recognized a voice when we did not. This could have happened due to the acoustic conditions under which we heard the voice. In addition, our sense of what direction and how far someone is away from us can also be fooled. To try this, have someone stand behind you and speak to you from a given side. Then take a paper tube and hold it up to the ear that is closest to the person. Have that person speak again. Surprisingly, the person now seems to be closer on the other side. That is because the sound waves need to travel farther to reach the ear. Thus, in measuring the time it takes the sound to be heard in both ears, the brain is tricked into thinking the person is actually closer to the other side.

This demonstrates that even the most complex machine, the human brain, can be fooled by sound and, in turn, by the human voice. If it is possible for the brain to be fooled, it seems only logical that a voice biometric can be fooled as well.

Not surprisingly, the use of voice biometrics for identification is often questioned. Can it deliver the same level of accuracy as other biometrics, and can it be deployed for use in a network security environment?

In our investigation of voice biometrics, we will try to answer these questions and provide a suitable background so that you can make the final decision.

To learn the most about voice biometrics, the discussion will be broken into the following areas:

- General description of voice biometrics
- How is the voice captured?
- Types of algorithms used for voice interpretation
- How can this biometric be spoofed?

General Description of Voice Biometrics

When we speak, words can be broken down into individual components known as phonemes. Each phoneme is delivered with pitch, cadence, and inflection. These three aspects of voice give each of us our unique voice sound. Even though we are all unique individuals and speak for ourselves, we can all sound very similar. This similarity can come from cultural and regional influences in the form of an accent; also, we learn certain inflections and pitches from our family. That is, if you spend enough time around someone, you can take on some of his/her voice characteristics. Not surprisingly, we have all at one time or another thought we heard one person speak when it was another.

The voice is a physiological and behavioral biometric. That is, it is influenced by our body and the environment we are in. For example, as children grow and pass through puberty, the voice changes. As we grow older, the voice takes on other nuances. Additionally, the sound of our voice can be different if we are talking in a large opera hall or a phone booth, as both have a very unique set of acoustics that will affect the sound of our voice. Therefore, it is possible that our voice does not always sound exactly the same. This again raises the question of the use of voice as an acceptable biometric for network security.

As discussed, the voice can change based on physiological factors and also environmental factors. Thus, both need to be taken into account when evaluating voice-based biometrics.

How Is the Voice Captured?

The voice can be captured either through the use of dedicated resources or existing infrastructure. An example of a dedicated resource is a stick microphone attached to a computer. Existing infrastructure can take the form of a telephone.

The use of either type of capture device is influenced by two qualities. The first is the physical quality of the device, and the second is the environment in which the sample is being taken.

For a microphone connected to a computer, the higher the quality, the better. As the quality of the microphone improves, its dynamic range increases, as does the quality of the components being used. It may also include some noise-reducing technologies to remove background ambient noise. If it is a multidirectional microphone, it is more likely to pick up background noise. If it is unidirectional, then it will normally take only sound waves originating from a particular spatial region.

Most phone sets are normally just sufficient for voice conversations. They can have poor microphones in the mouthpiece, or be of older, less advanced technology. In addition, the housing of the handset may introduce noise and distortion. The set itself may not even be digital. If it is analog, then the raw signal propagated down the line will be susceptible to line noise and distortion. The use of a digital set would convert analog signals to digital signals before transmitting. In this way, the quality of the voice signal can be maintained, as its digital representation will be used as input to the recognition algorithm. Like a microphone, ambient noise can affect the quality of the capture. Again, the use of a unidirectional microphone can help with this. It is generally not advisable to do voice biometrics with a speakerphone!

With the prevalence of wireless phone technology, these could also be used as capture devices for voice biometrics. Since the signal needs to travel through the open air and then to terrestrial lines, it is very susceptible to interference. With the current analog cellular technology, the quality of the voice can approach that of tin cans and string. The quality of the sound and signal is significantly improved with the newer digital cellular technology, which may make it a viable source for voice biometrics.

Types of Algorithms Used for Voice Interpretation

Now that we know what constitutes the voice biometric and how it can be captured, we need to know what types of algorithms are used. The algorithms used to match and enroll the voice biometric fall into the following general categories:[1]

---

1. The list of voice algorithms comes from Biometric Security Australia (*www.biometricsecurity.com.au/technologies/technologies.htm*).

- Fixed phrase verification
- Fixed vocabulary verification
- Flexible vocabulary verification
- Text-independent verification

Fixed phrase verification

As the name implies, the user both enrolls and verifies using a fixed phrase. This makes it easy for the user to enroll, as only one phrase may need to be repeated for enrollment. This type of verification is often viewed as simply comparing two wave forms. If they match within a tolerance, then they are assumed to be the same person and access is granted. The matching of the two wave forms is normally done using dynamic time warping.

Dynamic time warping is used to prepare for a comparison. An explanation of it is included here as background information. The algorithm attempts to solve the problem of comparing a reference template to a comparison template when the cadence of a phoneme is different. It accomplishes this using relatively simple mathematics. By minimizing the distance between the two signals, it is hoped that the templates can be accurately compared. To do this, each signal is mapped onto a local distance matrix. This is done by taking the absolute value of two cells at the same reference time. Thus, the matrix now contains an array of relative distances between the two signals. Next, an accumulated distance matrix is created. In doing so, a representative value is placed in each cell that is made up of its relative value and the lowest value of its nearest neighbor from the local distance matrix. Once the accumulated distance matrix is created, the shortest path is calculated. Once this path is determined, it can be used as a warping function to compare the two signals. In this way, the signals are now relatively time-synchronized for comparison.[2]

Fixed vocabulary verification

Fixed vocabulary verification is based on the user's being enrolled and verified from a known pool of words. This pool of words is usually made up of the digits 0 through 9, and some other randomly related words. For the user to enroll, each word in the vocabulary is repeated so that a unique user model is created. When it is time for the user to verify, he/she is prompted with a random subset of the vocabulary. When

---

2. *Ibid.*

the live template is compared to the enrolled template, a match is determined based on the breakdown of each word in the vocabulary relative to the enrolled word model. The match of each word model is summed to generate a value for determining a match.

Flexible vocabulary verification

Flexible vocabulary verification is based on the user's being able to use any word in a given lexicon for authentication. To accomplish this, the user is required to repeat a series of words from the lexicon that covers all the phonemes used in the lexicon. Not only does there have to be coverage of the entire set of phonemes, but the phonemes must also be tested in conjunction with each other. When the user needs to authenticate, he/she speaks any word or words from the lexicon. The words are then broken down into their individual phoneme components and compared.

Text-independent verification

Text-independent verification offers the promise of freedom to use any chosen phrase or words for authentication. To enroll, the user is free to say anything. Thus, when the user goes to verify, he/she is verified against all the other speaker models that have been created. Since this technique is generally considered weak, it is used in conjunction with continuous speaker monitoring. The user is constantly measured against all the other models. Since this method relies on continuous speech, it is not a useful method for biometric network security. It is included here for the sake of completeness.

Which Algorithm Is Best?

The decision of which algorithm would be best for voice biometrics should be based on a balance between convenience and security. Each algorithm has its own inherent tradeoffs. Thus, selecting which one to use is a risk management decision. If a company is more concerned with user convenience, then it should pick an algorithm that is easy to use and enroll. If a company is more concerned with security, then an algorithm that requires more in-depth enrollment and a wider variety of words/phrases for authentication should be considered.

Recommended Voice Algorithm

In this case, the algorithm I recommend offers a good tradeoff between convenience and security. Fixed vocabulary verification can use any word in the lexicon by itself or in combination with others. It does require the user to do a one-time enrollment for each word. This enrollment may require the user to repeat each word three to ten times, depending on the underlying algorithm implementation. Though this can be tedious, it is done only once, and then it can be leveraged many times over.

How Can This Biometric Be Spoofed?

As discussed in the opening of this chapter, it was accepted that even humans can be fooled into thinking we recognize a voice when we do not. If this is the case, it is believable and to be expected that a voice biometric system could be fooled as well. While it is generally accepted that voice biometrics do not provide the same level of FAR as other biometrics, voice biometrics offer other very attractive attributes such as high user acceptance and low hardware cost. The term "low cost" is relative to the quality of the identification and thus the ability to successfully enroll and verify. This is based on the ambient noise in the verification and enrollment location and the quality demanded by the underlying algorithm. It is ideal to use the same type of enrollment and verification device. This way, acoustical differences between different enrollment and verification devices can be minimized.

Voice biometrics are like any other biometric: susceptible to some level of spoofing. Attacks on a voice biometric system fall into the following categories:

- Attacking the physical voice
- Using artifacts
- Attacking the communications (see Chapter 5)
- Compromising the template (see Chapter 5)
- Attacking the fallback system (see Chapter 5)

Attacking the Physical Voice

During the discussion of which algorithm to pick, it was noted that a decision had to be made between user convenience and security. After evaluating the tradeoffs, if the company's decision was for convenience, then the system is much more susceptible to things like replay attacks from a recorded voice or voice impersonation. If, on the other hand, security won out over convenience, then the system is stronger and less likely to be compromised.

In general, attacks on voice biometrics either involve the playback of a static phrase or the spoofer's trying to impersonate the user.

Using artifacts

The artifacts used for voice biometrics are not of the same type as those used for other biometrics. Since there is no residual contact left from the templating, the artifacts need to be recorded. These recorded artifacts, that is, the users' voices, are then used as the basis for an attack. Once this is done, the artifacts, in effect, are used as described above in "Attacking the Physical Voice."

Mitigating this attack

The best mitigation for this type of attack is to use an algorithm that has a sufficiently large lexicon. The lexicon should also use less common words along with the standard digits. This way, it is less likely in normal conversation to use one of the special words from the lexicon.

Another countermeasure can be to have challenge phrases presented to the user to say in a limited amount of time. This way, the spoofer would need to have the lexicon recorded for the particular user and be able to produce the challenge words in the required amount of time.

Conclusion

Voice biometrics present an interesting option for biometric network security. They offer relative ease of use with also relatively cheap hardware. The biometric is not invasive to the user and is used on a daily basis. The drawbacks are the possible amount of enrollment to have a strong enough lexicon to use and the susceptibility of the biometric to impact from both environmental and physiological conditions, like catching a cold. As such, to accommodate for these drawbacks, the choice of FAR versus FRR needs to balanced. Again, it is a question of convenience versus security. In my opinion, there are biometrics better suited to network authentication than voice biometrics.

8

Iris Biometric Technology[1]

The use of the iris for biometric authentication is relatively new. All the current commercial algorithms are based on the original patented algorithm from John Daugman at the University of Cambridge. In 1994, the iris engine was ready and available for licensing. Since then, Iridian Technologies has purchased the algorithms and associated rights. Iridian Technologies has licensed other companies to build applications that leverage the iris algorithms.

Iris biometrics offer the promise of the Holy Grail of biometrics. A strong, reliable biometric trait is measured, generating a template that is simple to compare and provides virtually no FAR. There is also an extremely low FRR of 0.2% in three attempts.

With a very high FAR and a very low FRR, iris biometrics work very well for both identification and verification. It is clear that the iris can deliver the best level of accuracy of all other biometrics. However, the question remains: Can it be deployed for use in a network security environment?

In our investigation of iris biometrics, we will try to answer this question and provide a suitable background so that you can make a final decision.

To learn the most about iris biometrics, the discussion will be broken into the following areas:

- General description of iris biometrics
- How is the iris captured?

---

1. The entire reference for this chapter is taken from John Daugman's Web site (*www.cl.cam.ac.uk/users/jgd1000/*).

117

- How do the algorithms work?
- How can this biometric be spoofed?

General Description of Iris Biometrics

The iris is the only internally visible organ of the human body. It is located in the eye behind the cornea and aqueous humour, and it is an ideal trait for measurement. It is protected by the eyelid and cornea, and is not exposed to harsh conditions that may cause it to be difficult to image. The iris, like the fingerprint, forms during the early stages of fetal development and is completed by the eighth month. It is extremely distinctive and will not be the same even for genetically identical twins.

How Is the Iris Captured?

The iris is visible to the naked eye as a mosaic of texture. This is what is seen when the visible spectrum of light is used to illuminate the iris. When light from the near infrared regions is used, "slowly modulated stromal features are seen to dominate the iris."[2] It is these features that can be imaged up to one meter away with appropriate technology. The technology normally involves a monochromatic CCD camera in the 480 x 640 resolution range. This is used to extract an image frame of approximately 100–140 pixels in radius to capture the iris sufficiently.

For a user to have his/her iris captured, he/she needs to look into a camera and receive feedback on whether to move the camera up, down, left, right, closer, or farther away. Once the camera is appropriately positioned, a frame is captured and the iris is localized.

Description of the Iris Algorithm

Now that we know what constitutes the iris biometric, and how it can be captured, we need to know how the algorithm works.

Once an iris is captured, it is then converted into a template that is 2,048 bits in length. To compare a live template to the reference template, a simple exclusive OR (XOR) operation is done on the two values. Their corresponding mask bit vectors are used in an AND operation to verify that there were no artifacts affecting the comparison.

---

2. John Daugman, "How Iris Recognition Works," University of Cambridge, p. 2.

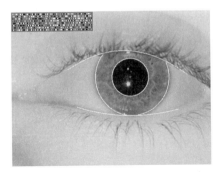

Figure 8–1
Sample of iris templating and resulting iris code.

The norms of the resulting XOR and AND operations are used to compute a Hamming Distance.[3] The Hamming Distance is a measure of dissimilarity between the two iris templates. This distance is then used to determine whether there is a match or not. Since there are many degrees of freedom in the iris code, a relatively large Hamming Distance can be used to still guarantee a near-zero FAR. This simplicity of the algorithm allows for very fast matching in the range of 100,000 per second on a 300MHz machine.

Figure 8–1 illustrates a sample of iris templating and the resulting iris code is shown in the top left of the image.

How Can This Biometric Be Spoofed?

The iris is an extremely difficult trait to spoof, yet there have been attempts at spoofing. There is little doubt that others will try and, given enough time, money, and energy, they may be successful. Attacks on the iris biometric fall into the following categories:

- Attacking the physical iris
- Using artifacts
- Attacking the communications (see Chapter 5)
- Compromising the template (see Chapter 5)
- Attacking the fallback system (see Chapter 5)

---

3. John Daugman, "How Iris Recognition Works," University of Cambridge, p. 4.

Attacking the Physical Iris

One attempt at spoofing was made by C'T of Germany. In its spoof, the company printed a high-quality digital image of an iris onto paper. The pupil area was then cut out so the spoofer could present his/her pupils along with the faked iris image. C'T succeeded in getting the system to capture an image and successfully authenticate.[4] This spoof was possible due to the robustness of the iris algorithm. The algorithm was designed to image an iris of any size.

Mitigating this attack

To mitigate against this particular attack, a check was added to the algorithm to look for a telltale signature created by the printing process and observed during the two-dimensional Fourier power spectrum analysis.

Using Artifacts

The artifacts used for iris biometrics are not of the same type as those used for other biometrics. Since there is no residual contact left from the templating, the artifact (the iris) needs to be recorded. The only recorded artifact, that is, the user's iris, must be used as the basis for an attack. Once this is done, the artifact, in effect, is used as described in "Attacking the Physical Iris."

Conclusion

Iris biometrics appear to offer the Holy Grail of biometrics. Iris biometrics are quick, robust, fast to compare, and resist spoofing better than any other trait So, this should be the ideal biometric for network security. From a pure technological standpoint, it is the clear winner, hands down. The last question to be answered is: Why has the iris biometric not overtaken every other biometric and been widely deployed? The reasons are quite simple:

1. Hardware cost—Specialized cameras are still required. These cameras need to have their own unique light source. As such, there are only certain economies of scale that can be leveraged to reduce the cost of the hardware. Continued research in this area will yield lower-cost products.

---

4. This section is based on the work from C'T (*www.heise.de/ct/english/02/11/114/*), Nov. 2002, p. 114.

2. User perception—Even though it is quite clear that the infrared light being used is perfectly safe, the mere thought of something being shined into the eye is disconcerting to the user.

3. Placement—To get the iris in the proper position takes a fair amount of coordination. Therefore, some users will never be able to use the product, and others will require longer times to become fully habituated to its use. Some cameras use eye recognition techniques to try to auto-pan and focus the camera. These solutions, while better, do increase the cost of the camera and may still require some user coordination.

4. Size—While the current size of the camera has been reduced to that of a desktop camera on steroids, it is still rather large. As the camera decreases in size, it will become easier to find the required desk real estate for its deployment.

All of the above problems will be solved with time, money, and technological advances. When this happens and user perception can be changed, iris technology will be a strong competitor to fingerprint biometrics for network security.

Part 3

IMPLEMENTING BIOMETRICS FOR NETWORK SECURITY

9

Recommended Biometric for Network Security

In the previous chapters, we explored finger, face, voice, and iris biometrics. We examined each biometric's strengths and weaknesses, and we looked at what types of algorithms are available. Also, Chapter 4 described the qualities that make a biometric technology good for network security. Now that we have examined both the biometrics that could be suitable for network access and their qualities, a recommendation of which technology to use needs to be made.

The recommendation put forth here is made with the best technologies available at the time. As biometric technology advances, some of the analyses here will need to be revisited. What will remain solid is the methodology used to evaluate which biometric system best meets the needs for network security.

Chapter 4 outlined the following as characteristics of a good biometric for network security:

- Users willingly accept the biometric device
- Users find it easy to use
- Total technology costs and benefits provide a suitable ROI
- Technology is deployable and supportable
- Technology is not invasive and requires the user to actively submit to its use
- Technology is mature and reliable
- Users become habituated quickly to the device

For the biometrics examined, a score of 0 to 10 was assigned for each characteristic. An ideal biometric was defined as having a perfect score of 10 in each category. What follows is the examination of each biometric type and the reasoning for the scores it received.

Finger Biometrics

The finger biometric scored very well relative to the ideal biometric, as shown in Figure 9–1. Its greatest strengths are its deployability and maturity. The greatest weakness comes from the cost and hence ROI. What follows is a breakdown of each characteristic for the finger biometric.

Acceptance: 9

Finger biometrics are some of the oldest and most studied methods of biometric identification. People accept them because of their long history. It also helps that finger biometrics are active, which means that the user needs to submit to the biometric system for sampling. It does not

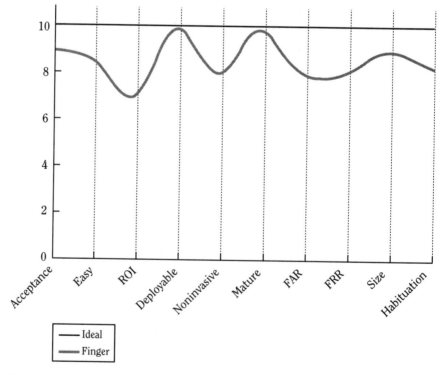

Figure 9–1
Scores for finger biometrics.

qualify for ideal status because some people feel that using their finger-print is very similar to being fingerprinted for a criminal offense.

Easy: 8.5

The ease of use of finger biometrics has increased greatly. The new sensors available and the use of better ergonomics have led to this increase in ease of use. Some devices may not be optimal for use with all fingers, and others may not work well with all finger types.

ROI: 7

The decreasing cost of devices and the ease of deployment and training make this a very cost-effective technology. With biometrics being used for password replacement or as a strong factor of authentication for SSO, the savings alone on password resets present a very attractive ROI.

Deployable: 9.9

Deployability considers how easy it is to get a device on a desktop. Finger biometric devices for network security have become much smaller. USB connections have freed the devices from having to use legacy serial or parallel ports and the associated hassles that come from using those connection methods.

Noninvasive: 8

Since finger biometrics are associated with active devices, and they image only an exterior feature, they are much more noninvasive than many other biometric methods. A higher score was not given since many feel that fingerprints are very private due to the fact that they are used by law enforcement. This can mean that there is some stigma associated with using finger-based biometrics.

Mature: 9.9

As stated in the opening, fingerprint biometrics are some of the oldest and most studied biometrics. This continued study and time on the market have allowed the fingerprint biometric to mature to a point where the research in the field has turned to increasingly difficult features to implement.

FAR: 8

The FAR measurement is somewhat important depending on the reason for deployment. A deployment done for convenience would want the FAR to be set where the majority of the users can authenticate at a meaningful level. If security is the primary concern, then an increase in FAR will lead to a decrease in user convenience.

FRR: 8

The FRR measurement is somewhat important depending on the reason for deployment. A deployment done for convenience would want the FRR to be set as low as possible to still have some confidence in the verification and/or identification taking place.

Size: 9

Due to the limited desk space that most users have, it is not surprising to have to fight for desktop real estate. Again, through good design and maturity, this device has significantly reduced its physical footprint on the desktop.

Habituation: 8.5

A user can become habituated to a fingerprint biometric rather quickly. This stems from the fact that on a daily basis, we use our hands for everything, and so we have built up a fair amount of dexterity and coordination with them. The placing of a finger on a scanner is relatively straightforward, but it still requires a bit of coordination.

Face Biometrics

Face biometrics are being heavily researched. They offer the promise of high user acceptance. It seems natural to use your face for recognition since that is what we use everyday to recognize people. This biometric's greatest strengths are its noninvasiveness and user acceptance, as shown in Figure 9–2. The greatest weakness comes from the ROI characteristic. What follows is a breakdown of each characteristic for face biometrics.

Acceptance: 8.5

Face biometrics are natural to use. The method relies on the user presenting his/her face for recognition. In this way, it is something that users

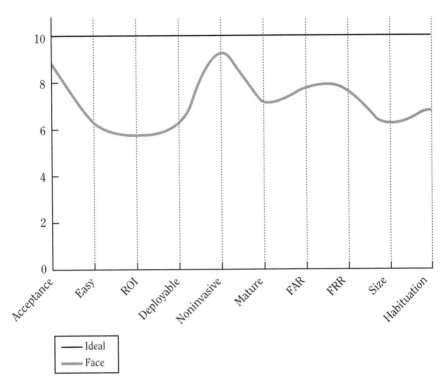

Figure 9–2
Scores for face biometrics.

do all the time. It is the face that is used to recognize a person the majority of the time. Using facial recognition has very wide acceptance. What prevents this biometric from having the same score as, or higher than, fingerprint biometrics is the fact that it is passive. That is, a face can be authenticated or identified without the user's consent, which makes some users do feel uncomfortable about the use of face biometrics.

Easy: 6

The ease of use of face biometrics is steadily increasing. As seen in Chapter 6, face biometrics can be very hard to use based on facial expression, lighting, head positioning, and physiological changes like beards and the part-time wearing of glasses. For this reason, it did not score as well in this category.

ROI: 5.5

While it is possible to use off-the-shelf camera technology for facial recognition, a more specialized camera should be used to get the high-quality pictures necessary for reliable use. These specialized cameras are currently not getting the economies of scale required to drive down their cost. In addition, when such a camera is deployed, there is a significant amount of time required to position the camera properly. It also needs to be secured to the work environment in such a way as to get the best field of view of each user's face. Additional lighting or changes to existing lighting may be required.

The above factors add higher costs through the specialized camera, plus the labor to get the camera deployed and functioning. This produces a longer period of time to obtain a good ROI.

Deployable: 6

A face biometric device for network security can be difficult to deploy. Based on the need for positioning the camera to capture the maximum field of view, plus adjusting for possible lighting conditions, it could be a time-consuming process. Once the camera is deployed, it would need to be tested and possibly re-adjusted to achieve maximum field of view. Over time, these restrictions will improve. If high-quality cameras are ever built into computer monitors, deployment will become much easier. The reason for this is that each user will have already adjusted the monitor in such a way that when he/she looks at the monitor, his/her face will be relatively close and normally centered in the viewing area.

The time needed for deployment and the other adjustments that may be needed make this technology more difficult to deploy.

Noninvasive: 9

Since face biometrics are so natural, users find them noninvasive. We are all comfortable with our face being used for recognition. A perfect score was not given since some may feel that face biometrics can be used as a passive tracking system. For this reason, it does not have the 100% acceptance that the ideal biometric would have. One way to increase acceptance to almost 100% is through the use of a privacy-positive biometric policy. This way, users would feel more comfortable with the technology's use.

Mature: 7

The use of facial identification has been around a long time. Any picture drawn or taken of the face provides a ready source for identification. The current trend for face biometrics is more for access control. Since the events of September 11, 2001, the desire for identification using faces has provided an expanding market for face biometrics. Because of this, the majority of the biometric research is being done in this area. As a result, less research is being done for using face biometrics for network access. Therefore, the face biometric area needs additional maturity.

FAR: 7.5

As seen in Chapter 4, there are a number of issues that can affect facial FAR. Face biometrics also have a higher spoofing factor than other biometrics. This leads to increasing the FAR as low as possible, which then has the effect of increasing the FRR. When compared to finger or iris biometrics, the face biometric needs to show more improvement in this area.

FRR: 7.5

With the fact that the FAR for face biometrics needs to be low enough to prevent spoofing, it will increase the FRR. In addition, the need for the user to present his/her face in just the right way will also increase the FRR. For this reason, the score for the FRR is not as high as for other biometrics.

Size: 6

The size of the specialized camera for face biometrics can be larger than a normal desktop video conferencing camera. Quite often, these cameras will have their own additional illumination, which requires them to be larger. For these reasons, the face biometric scored the way it did for this characteristic.

Habituation: 7.5

The use of face biometrics can require the user to be highly habituated. The user may need to present his/her face at the proper angle, with the right neutral expression, and hold relatively still. These requirements can be difficult, and so the time needed to become highly habituated could be fairly long.

Voice Biometrics

Voice biometrics, like face biometrics, are natural to use. When we cannot see someone but can hear him/her, that can be sufficient for us to recognize who it is. This biometric's greatest strengths are its size and noninvasiveness, as seen in Figure 9–3. The greatest weaknesses come from the FAR and FRR. What follows is a breakdown of each characteristic for voice biometrics.

Acceptance: 8.5

Voice biometrics rely on the user's speaking for recognition, which is obviously something that users do all the time. The voice biometric has

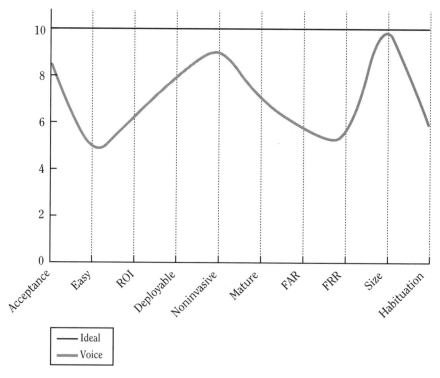

Figure 9–3
Scores for voice biometrics.

wide acceptance. What prevents it from having the same score as, or a higher score than, fingerprint biometrics is the fact that it is passive.

Easy: 5

The ease of use of voice biometrics needs to improve. The required time to train a system and enroll, coupled with the need for clear speech and low ambient noise, can make voice biometrics difficult to use. For this reason, it did not score well in this category.

ROI: 5.5

The cost of the hardware to use with voice biometrics is relatively low. A decent-quality microphone is relatively affordable. The cost of deploying the microphone is normally low, as most computers have sound cards with a microphone jack. What diminishes the ROI is the user's need to use the biometric daily. Voice biometrics can take a long time to train and enroll. They are also very susceptible to background noise and changes in the user's voice. For these reasons, many calls to the help desk could be generated, thus lowering the overall ROI.

Deployable: 8

A voice biometric for network security is relatively easy to deploy. The microphone needs only to be plugged into the sound card of the user's machine. That is relatively quick and easy to do. Once the microphone is deployed, it needs to be tested and possibly re-adjusted to minimize background noise.

Since additional time is needed for testing and placement of the microphone, voice biometrics scored slightly lower than finger biometrics.

Noninvasive: 9

Since the voice biometric is natural, users find it noninvasive. We are all comfortable with using our voice for recognition. A perfect score was not given since some may feel that voice biometrics can be used as a passive tracking system. For this reason, it does not have the 100% acceptance that the ideal biometric would have. One way to increase acceptance to almost 100% is through the use of a privacy-positive biometric policy. This way, the users would feel more comfortable with the technology's use.

Mature: 7

The use of voice identification has been around a long time. We are accustomed to using the sound of other peoples' voices to identify them. However, the use by machines of voice biometrics is relatively new and still needs additional research and time for it to mature.

FAR: 6

As discussed in Chapter 7, for any biometric, you must decide on the tradeoff between security and user convenience based on the algorithm chosen. The voice biometric is also fairly susceptible to spoofing attacks.

For the above reasons, voice biometrics scored low on the FAR measurement.

FRR: 5.5

For voice biometrics, there can be a very high FRR. This is due to the nature of the biometric. The voice changes over time, and can also vary from hour to hour depending on physical health and the ambient environment. Ambient noise can cause the FRR to increase. The enrollment procedure can also lead to an increased FRR. If the enroller and user were not diligent enough in their training of the voice system, the user could have a very hard time authenticating.

Size: 9.9

The size of the microphone is very small and will use almost minimal real estate on the desktop. It did not score as high as the ideal biometric, however, since something still needed to be deployed.

Habituation: 7.5

The use of voice biometrics can require the user to be highly habituated. The user needs to present his/her voice at the right pitch, tempo, and cadence. These things can be difficult for people to do, so the time needed to be come habituated to the degree required could be relatively long.

Iris Biometrics

Iris biometrics offer the biggest "cool" factor of all the biometrics. Iris biometrics are most often seen in spy movies, and are associated with securing only the most important data. When it comes to its use as a biometric for network security, some shortcomings are evident, yet other characteristics of iris biometrics are very attractive. Its greatest strengths lay in the FRR and FAR, as seen in Figure 9–4. The greatest weakness comes from being highly invasive. What follows is a breakdown of each characteristic for iris biometrics.

Acceptance: 4

Even though iris biometrics have a high cool factor, users are less accepting of them. The main reason for this is the perceived invasive

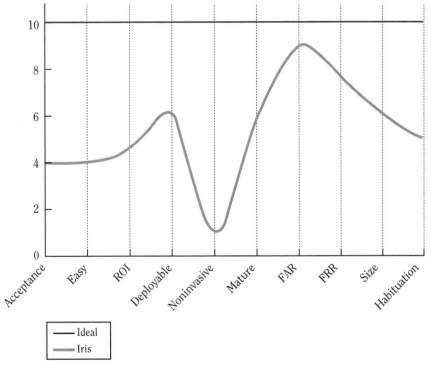

Figure 9–4
Scores for iris biometrics.

nature of the biometric. Users have a hard time coming to grips with a light being shined into their eyes. It is the fear of injury to the eye that increases their uneasiness.

Easy: 4

Since the biometric in use is actually internal to the body, the positioning and relative closeness of the user to the reader are very high. Also, the need to perfectly align the eye with the scanner is required, which can cause some dexterity issues for users.

ROI: 4.5

The cost of the hardware needed for iris biometrics is relatively high. The camera needs to have a specialized light source to properly illuminate the iris. This does not lend itself well to achieving economies of scale. Also, the level of dexterity required to use the camera and the relative reluctance of the users to use it produce a high-cost/low-savings environment.

Deployable: 6

The iris biometric for network security is very similar to the face biometric for deployment. Unlike a face biometric camera, an iris biometric camera is not as susceptible to ambient lighting conditions. It does require a fair amount of desktop real estate, and it needs to be mounted so that the user is very comfortable with its use. This can require the installer to spend time fine-tuning the camera position for each user.

Noninvasive: 1

Iris biometrics without question are the most invasive. The very nature of the biometric being used contributes to this fact. It should be noted that most of the insistence that iris biometrics are invasive is purely user perception. Perception can be changed over time with education and more widespread use. If the iris biometric is to make it big in network access, this is one area that will need to be overcome.

Mature: 6

Even though iris biometrics have been commercially available for only about a decade, they are relatively mature. The research behind the use of the iris, and the simplicity and strength of the algorithm, lead to a relatively high maturity score. Where the iris biometric needs additional maturity is in the areas of user acceptance and hardware cost reduction.

FAR: 9

The FAR of the iris biometric is second to none. It is very robust and reliable. In the tens of millions of comparisons done in testing, not one false acceptance was seen. No biometric will ever match the ideal criteria. Since the FAR is a measure of probability, and it is used in conjunction with the law of large numbers, there is bound to eventually be a false acceptance.

FRR: 7.5

For the very reasons that give iris biometrics an incredible FAR, the same holds true for the FRR. The majority of the FRR is normally caused by user error in placement of the iris for recognition. This difficulty in placement is what drives down the score of the iris biometric. These failures can also be called *failures to acquire*. If a failure to acquire occurs during verification, it can then cause the user to be falsely rejected.

Size: 6

The size of the camera needed for iris biometrics is relatively large. Like face biometrics, the camera requires a fair amount of desktop real estate for deployment.

Habituation: 5

The use of iris biometrics can require the user to be highly habituated. The user needs to present the iris to the camera in just the right way. This can be difficult to do, as the user may have a hard time holding his/her head still, or may have a slight fear of light being shined into the eye. This could cause a person to not be as confident in their placement as he/she should be.

The Choice of a Biometric for Network Access

As seen in this chapter, each biometric was evaluated for its suitability for network security and scores were given for each characteristic. Fig-

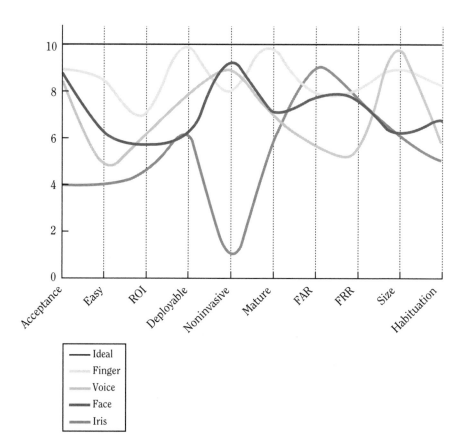

Figure 9–5
Scores for all biometrics.

ure 9–5 contains a graph showing all the individual graphs together. Here, it is very easy to see how a particular biometric performed relative to the other biometrics.

It is clear from Figure 9–5 that the closest overall to being ideal is the fingerprint biometric. This is also what is being seen in the marketplace. Fingerprint biometrics are clearly deployed more than any other type of biometric solution. The reasons for this are their overall general suitability for use and their robustness.

Conclusion

What we started in an earlier chapter as a general discussion on biometrics for network security has concluded with a choice of the best biometric for network security. This choice was based on the score that each biometric received based on the characteristics of an ideal biometric. While the iris biometric proved to be the most secure, and voice and face biometrics had the highest levels of user acceptance, it was the fingerprint biometric that offered the best overall solution.

10

An Introduction
to Statistical
Measures
of Biometrics

To know how well something performs, we must be able to quantify the performance. For automobiles, we measure gas consumption; for heating and cooling units, we measure effectiveness in British thermal units (BTUs). Biometrics have their own similar performance measures.

To know if a car is getting good fuel economy or if a heater or air conditioner is doing its job, we look at what the statistics mean. We then compare them to our expectations or some other accepted norm. At no time does knowing how the performance measure was calculated impact our ability to evaluate performance. Similarly, for biometrics, how a performance measure is calculated is of little value. There are exceptions to this statement, which will be discussed. In general, just knowing what a performance measurement means is sufficient. For our purposes, the statistical measures to be used for biometrics are:

- FAR (False Acceptance Rate)
- FRR (False Rejection Rate)
- FTE (Failure to Enroll)
- EER (Equal Error Rate)

A discussion of each statistical measure follows.

FAR

Definition

The FAR is defined as the probability that a user making a false claim about his/her identity will be verified as that false identity. For example, if Matt types Chris' user ID into the biometric login for Chris' PC, Matt has just made a false claim that he is Chris. Matt presents his biometric measurement for verification. If the biometric system matches Matt to Chris, then there is a false acceptance. This could happen because the matching threshold is set too high, or it could be that Matt's biometric feature is very similar to Chris'. Either way, a false acceptance has occurred.

The Simple Math

When the FAR is calculated by a biometrics vendor, it is generally very straightforward. Using our example, it is equal to the number of times that Matt has successfully authenticated as Chris divided by his total number of attempts. In this case, Chris is referred to as the "MatchUser" and Matt as the "NonMatchUser." The simple math formula for this looks like the following, where n represents a number to uniquely identify each user:

$n = enrolleduser$

n	$value$
1	$Chris$
2	$Matt$

$NonMatchUser'(n) = NumberofNonMatchUserSuccessfulAuthentications$
$NonMatchUser(n) = NumberofNonMatchUserAttemptsToFalselyAuthenticate$
$FAR\ (n) = NonMatchUser'(n)/NonMatchUser(n)$

$n = 1$

$FAR\ (Chris)\ /\ Matt\ (Chris)$

This gives us the basis for Matt and Chris. What if we have another user, David? We could say that Matt and Chris are representative of our user population and just assume that the FAR will be the same for David. Statistically, the more times something is done, the greater the confidence in the result. Thus, to ensure a high probability that the FAR we calculate is statistically significant, we would need to do this for every combination of users we have. We would need to take all the calculated FARs for each user's attempt to falsely authenticate as another, sum them up, and divide by the total number of users. For example, we could take the above formulas and do them over again for each user. We would eventually get something that looks like the following:

$$FAR\ (Chris) = (Matt'(Chris)\ /\ Matt(Chris) + David'(Chris)\ /\ David(Chris))\ /\ 2$$

If we generalize the formula, we get:

$n = enrolleduser$
$N = totalenrolleduserpopulation$
$NonMatchUser'(n) = NumberOfNonMatchUserssuccessfulAuthentication$
$NonMatchUser(n) = Numberof NonMatchUserAttemptsToFalselyAuthenticate$

n	$value$
1	Chris
2	Matt
3	David
4	Craig
5	Peter
.	.
N	Victoria

$$FAR(n) = NonMatchUser'(n)\ /\ NonMatchUser(n)$$

$$FAR = 1\ /\ N \sum_{n=1}^{N} FAR(n)$$

Why Is This Important?

The importance of the FAR is the strength of the matching algorithm. The stronger the algorithm, the less likely that a false authentication will happen. Matt has a greater chance of falsely authenticating as Chris at 1:500 than he does at 1:10,000. An example of this would be playing a ring-toss game. In this game, the object is to throw a ring on to a particular peg. The ring represents Matt's false authentication attempt. The number of pegs represents the strength of the biometric algorithm. The gameboard itself represents Chris' biometric enrollment. In the first case, there are 500 pegs on which to throw the ring. The peg that needs to be ringed for a winner is not marked. Thus, Matt has a 1 in 500 chance of hitting the right peg. Now, if Matt is playing the same game, but this time there are 10,000 pegs in the same area, Matt now has a 1 in 10,000 chance of hitting the right peg.

Carrying this example further, Chris now needs to authenticate. He knows the layout of the board and what ring to toss his peg onto. He knows this because he is really who he says he is. In the first game, he is faced with 500 pegs. Chris knows what peg to toss his ring onto in order to get authenticated. There is a chance he could miss, which is very low. If at any time Chris does not hit his peg, then he is falsely rejected. That is to say, he has not been authenticated as himself, even though he is Chris.

FRR

Definition

The *FRR* is defined as the probability that a user making a true claim about his/her identity will be rejected as him/herself. For example, if Chris types his correct user ID into the biometric login for his PC, Chris has just made a true claim that he is Chris. Chris presents his biometric measurement for verification. If the biometric system does not match Chris to Chris, then there is a false rejection. This could happen because the matching threshold is set too low, or Chris' presented biometric feature is not close enough to the biometric template. Either way, a false rejection has occurred.

The Simple Math

When the FRR is calculated by a biometric vendor, it is generally very straightforward. Again, using our example, it is equal to the number of times that Chris unsuccessfully authenticated as Chris divided by his total number of attempts. In this case, Chris is referred to as the "MatchUser":

$n = enrolleduser$
$N = totalenrolleduserpopulation$

n	value
1	Chris
2	Matt

MatchUser'(n) = NumberofMatchUserUnSuccessfulAuthentications
MatchUser(n) = NumberofMatchUserAttemptsToAuthenticate
FRR (n) = MatchUser'(n)/MatchUser(n)

n = 1

FRR (Chris) = Chris'(Chris) / Chris(Chris)

This gives us the basis for Chris' FRR. What if we have another user, Matt? We could say that Chris is representative of our user population and just assume that the FRR will be the same for Matt. Statistically, the more times something is done, the greater the confidence in the result. Thus, if we want to ensure a high probability that the FRR we calculate is statistically significant, we would need to do this for every user. We would then need to take all the calculated FRRs for each user's attempt to authenticate as himself/herself, sum them up, and divide by the total number of users. The result is the mean (average) FRR for all users of a system. For example, we would take the above formulas and compute them for each user. We would eventually get something that looks like the following:

FRR(N) (Chris'(Chris) / Chris(Chris) + Matt'(Matt) / Matt(Matt)) / 2

If we generalize the formula, we get:

n = enrolleduser
N = totalenrolleduserpopulation
MatchUser'(n) = NumberOfMatchUserUnsuccessfulAuthentication
MatchUser(n) = NumberofMatchUserAttemptsToAuthenticate

n	*value*
1	*Chris*
2	*Matt*
3	*David*
4	*Craig*
5	*Peter*
.	.
N	*Victoria*

$$FRR(n) = NonMatchUser'(n) / NonMatchUser(n)$$

$$FRR = 1 / N \sum_{n=1}^{N} FRR(n)$$

Why Is This Important?

The strength of the FRR is the robustness of the algorithm. The more accurate the matching algorithm, the less likely a false rejection will happen. Chris has a lower chance of being falsely rejected as himself at 1:500 than he does at 1:10,000. Again, let's use the example of playing a ring-toss game. In this game, the ring represents Chris' authentication attempt. The distance between the pegs represents the robustness of the biometric algorithm. The gameboard itself represents Chris' biometric enrollment. In the first case, there are 500 pegs on which to throw the ring. The peg that needs to be ringed for a winner is known. Thus, Chris has a 1 in 500 chance of hitting the right peg. Chris also has less of a chance of hitting the wrong peg since there is generous spacing between the pegs. Now, if Chris plays the same game, but this time there are 10,000 pegs in the same area, he has a 1 in 10,000 chance of hitting the right peg. There is now also less spacing between pegs, as the playing area is the same size as it was for 500 pegs. So, Chris has a greater chance of landing on the wrong peg because of the pegs' relative proximity to each other.

FTE

Definition

The FTE is defined as the probability that a user attempting to biometrically enroll will be unable to. For example, Craig goes to the group in his company responsible for biometric enrollments. He is quickly instructed on the use of a biometric device, and then he attempts to have his biometric trait enrolled. At this time, he is unable to be enrolled. What defines his FTE can influence this measure. If the FTE is defined as a single-attempt failure, then the FTE will likely be higher than what would be seen over a larger group of people.

The FTE is normally defined by a minimum of three attempts. This is justified by the *Rule of Three*. The Rule of Three in this case provides us with a confidence level for a given error rate for our FTE. It also assumes that each attempt to enroll is independent, identically distributed, and that the user population size is significantly large enough. For example, if Craig is part of a population of 300 people, then using the Rule of Three for a 95% confidence level, we would obtain an FTE of 1%.[1] Thus, if Craig is still unable to be enrolled after three attempts, he has had an FTE.

The Simple Math

When the FTE is calculated by a biometric vendor, it is generally calculated with three attempts for enrollment. Since multiple attempts may need to occur before a decision is made on a success or failure, the three or fewer attempts will be called an enrollment event. In this case, a successful enrollment event occurs if Craig can be enrolled in three or fewer attempts. An unsuccessful enrollment event occurs if Craig, on his third attempt, is still unsuccessful. Thus, the FTE is calculated as the number of unsuccessful enrollment events divided by the total number of enrollment events.

$$n = EnrollmentCandidate$$
$$N = TotalNumberofEnrollmentCandidates$$

n	value
1	Craig
2	Matt

$$Event'(n) = NumberofUnsuccessfulEnrollmentEvents$$
$$Event(n) = TotalNumberofEnrollmentEvents$$
$$FTE(n) = Event'(n) / Event(n)$$

$$n = 1$$

$$FTE\ (Craig) = Event'(Craig) / Event(Craig)$$

This gives us the basis for Craig's FTE. What if we have another user, Matt? We could say that Craig is representative of our user population and just assume that the FTE will be the same for Matt. Statistically, the more times something is done, the greater the confidence in

---

1. A.J. Mansfield and J.L. Wayman, Best Practices in Testing and Reporting Performance of Biometric Devices Version 2.01 (Queens Road, Teddington, Middlesex, UK: Centre of Mathematics and Scientific Computing National Physical Laboratory), August 2002, p. 11.

the result. Thus, if we want to have a high confidence that the FTE we calculate is statistically significant, we would need to do this for every user. We would then need to take all the calculated FTEs for each user's attempt to biometrically enroll, sum them up, and divide by the total of all biometric enrollment attempts to determine the mean (average) FTE. For example, we could take the above formulas and do them over again for each user. We would eventually get something that looks like the following:

$$FTE(N) = (Event'(Craig) \,/\, Event(Craig) + Event'(Matt) \,/\, Event(Matt)) \,/\, 2$$

If we generalize the formula, we get:

$n = EnrollmentCandidate$
$N = TotalNumberofEnrollmentCandidates$
$Event'(n) = NumberofUnsuccessfulEnrollmentEvents$
$Event(n) = TotalNumberofEnrollmentEvents$

n	value
1	Chris
2	Matt
3	David
4	Craig
5	Peter
.	.
N	Victoria

$$FTE(n) = event'(n) \,/\, Event(n)$$
$$FTE = 1\,/\,N \sum_{n=1}^{N} FTE(n)$$

Why Is This Important?

The strength of the FTE is the amount of coverage for the population that the biometric system has. The more coverage the biometric system has, the less likely that a user will experience an FTE. Craig has a greater chance of being enrolled in a biometric system that has greater coverage than one that does not. An example of this is playing golf. In this example, the ball is a biometric enrollment attempt. The par for the hole is 3, and it represents the number of attempts before an FTE occurs. The size of the green represents the coverage provided by the biometric system. If Craig is playing a par 3 hole on a green with large coverage, his probability of putting the ball on the green is very high, and thus he has a lower probability of not making par. If the hole being played has a green with little coverage, then the probability of putting the ball on the green is lower, and the probability of not making par is higher.

A Quick Note on Biometric Systems

In the FTE description, the measure is referenced to a biometric system. This biometric system is made up of the hardware to acquire the enrollment, the algorithm for templating and comparison, and the user. An FTE could be caused by 1, 2, or all 3 of these entities. For example, if the biometric hardware is malfunctioning or is not properly maintained, this could cause an FTE. An algorithm that is not tuned properly could also reject an enrollment event because of the lack of features present, or the presence of features that are not incorporated into the algorithm. A FTE could be caused by a user who does not have the physical dexterity to provide the biometric sample, or is slow to habituate to the system.

When examining a biometric system's FTE, try to eliminate the parts of the system that can be controlled. For example, have the equipment properly cleaned and serviced. Tune the algorithm for your needs. Lastly, try reducing the human factor by choosing devices that are ergonomic, providing additional assistance to the user during enrollment, and also have properly qualified people doing the enrollments. Taking these steps will help to reduce the FTE and also increase user confidence in the system itself.

EER

Definition

The EER is defined as the crossover point on a graph that has both the FAR and FRR curves plotted. The EER can also be calculated from a receiver operating characteristic (ROC) curve, which plots FAR against FRR to determine a particular device's sensitivity and accuracy. The choice of using the crossover point of the FRR/FAR or using a ROC is a question of significance. An EER calculated using the FRR and FAR is susceptible to manipulation based on the granularity of threshold values. A ROC-based EER is not affected by such manipulations because the FRR and FAR are graphed together. Thus, the EER calculated using a ROC is less dependent on scaling.[2]

The Simple Math

To calculate the EER using the FRR/FAR crossover, the following is done: For any given threshold value from 0 to 1, respective FAR and FRR are calculated and plotted on the same graph. Since the granularity used for the values between 0 and 1 can be selected, this introduces the possibility of manipulating the results. A sample graph would look like Figure 10–1.

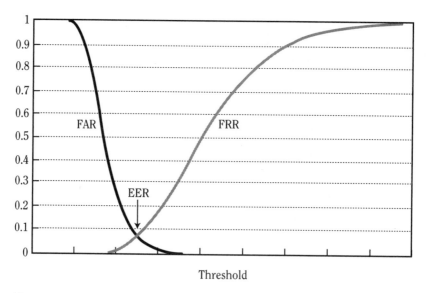

Figure 10–1
Calculating EER from FAR – FRR intersection.

2.   Dr. Manfred Bromba, BioIdentification Frequently Asked Questions (*http://www.bromba.com/faq/biofaqe.htm*).

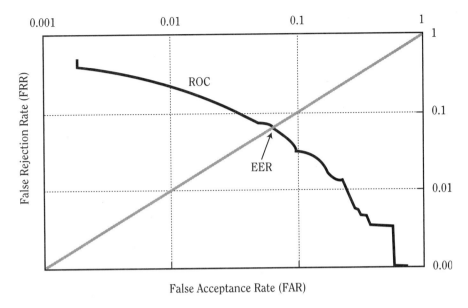

Figure 10–2
Calculating EER from a ROC curve.

As you can see from the graph, the EER occurs where the two lines cross.

To calculate the ROC of a biometric system, each corresponding FAR and FRR point is plotted on a logarithmic scale (Figure 10–2). The EER is then found by extending a 45-degree line from the point of origin (0,0). Where this line crosses the ROC is the EER. This happens because when the FRR has a value of 1, the FAR has a value of 0, and when the FRR has a value of 0, the FAR has a value of 1.

Why Is This Important?

The strength of the EER is that it gives a comparison of different biometric systems. That is, since biometric systems in general do not always offer the same threshold settings, it would be difficult to compare apples to apples. Thus, in comparing a normalized statistic like the EER, we can try to get some relative comparison of two biometric systems.

What Measure Is Most Important?

When looking at biometric systems, it is easy to get lost in all the statistical measures available. To decide what measure is most important to your choice of a biometric system, its use needs to be defined as follows:

- Define the user population.
- Is the application for verification or identification?
- Are other means of authentication available?
- What is the importance of the biometric authentication?
- Is it driven by convenience and ease of use?

Define the User Population

When implementing a biometric system, the user population needs to be defined based on age, profession, or other population-specific characteristics. If the population is skewed toward the elderly or very young, then there is a concern over the success of the enrollment. In this case, a biometric system with a low FTE would be the most appropriate choice, so that you can be assured that a large percentage of the population will be enrolled. Also, if the professions of the population could affect the ability to enroll (e.g., people who work with their hands may have a harder time using finger-based biometrics), the FTE needs to be the most important measure.

Is the Application for Verification or Identification?

The use of a biometric system can suggest what biometric measures should be most important. If the biometric system is going to be used for verification (i.e., users will make claims of their identity), then it is most important that false rejections are minimized. In this case, a system that provides a very low FRR would be best. The choice of the FRR is based on the fact that a one-to-one match must take place. By reducing the set of biometrics that may be falsely matched against, the FRR becomes the most important measure.

If the biometric system is going to be used for identification (i.e., the users are not making claims about their identity), false authentications are most important. In this case, a system that provides a very low FAR would be best. The choice of the FAR is based on that fact that it is more important to properly identify a user than to ensure that the user is not falsely rejected. The set of biometrics to be compared against cannot be pared down. Thus, we want to minimize the possibility of a false authentication, and so the FAR becomes the most important measure.

Are Other Means of Authentication Available?

It is well-known that for any biometric system implemented, 3–5% of the population base will not be able to use the system. If other authentication methods are not available or prove more costly to use and support, then another biometric system must be chosen that minimizes the exceptions. To minimize the exceptions, the system needs to be analyzed to see if the inability to use the system comes from the inability to enroll or to verify. If it is a case of not being able to enroll, then the FTE of the biometric system needs to be as low as possible. If it is a case of not being able to verify, then it is necessary to determine whether the exception threshold for authentication can be lowered. In this case, if the answer is yes, then we want a system with a lower FRR. This way, the user is less likely to be rejected.

What Is the Importance of the Biometric Authentication?

A biometric system controlling access to company secrets often requires a different biometric measure than a system controlling access to a user's personal address book. In the case where the biometric system is controlling access to sensitive information or a physical area, we should be more concerned about the FAR. In this case, the chance of the user's having to possibly attempt more authentications (and therefore decreasing user convenience) is of less importance than a false acceptance. If, on the other hand, the biometric system has been implemented for reasons of pure convenience only, then it is more important to minimize the FRR.

In the case where a biometric system is protecting something of importance and the user population is also demanding increased security, then the EER needs to be evaluated. This measure will give a good comparison of the tradeoff between convenience and security. Thus, the lower the EER, the more likely that the biometric system will meet the known requirements.

Is It Driven by Convenience and Ease of Use?

If a biometric system is driven by convenience and ease of use, then minimizing the FRR or having a low FTE becomes more important. Having a low FRR implies that the biometric system is willing to allow a higher level of false authentications. Having a low FTE means that more of the population will be able to use the biometric system as a convenience.

Conclusion

Statistical measures of biometrics can be used to decide which biometric system will best suit your needs. Not knowing the math behind a measurement should not impact one's ability to understand and compare the different statistical measures. The most important biometric statistical measures are:

- FAR–Measures the probability that an imposter will authenticate as a legitimate user.
- FRR–Measures the probability that a user who makes a legitimate claim about his/her identity will be falsely rejected.
- FTE–Measures the probability that an enrollment candidate will be unable to enroll in the biometric system.
- ERR–Measures the intrinsic strength of the biometric system and compares the strength of different biometric systems based on their EERs.

For each implementation, one or more of these biometric statistical measures can be important. To decide which ones are important, look at how the biometric system is going to be implemented, as well as how the user population is defined.

11

The Biometric Transaction

Privacy is a part of each person's individuality. Trusting someone means sharing some of that privacy with him/her. For sharing of private information to occur, there must be security and confidence in the relationship. Security and confidence can be gained over time as a result of shared experiences.

A biometric trait is a very private matter. It is something unique to an individual and has great value. A biometric trait, unlike an issued identifier like a social security number, cannot be changed. This means that the use of the biometric trait should be treated with the utmost privacy. This privacy is supplied by securing the entire biometric transaction.

The value of a biometric trait is that it can be used to identify the owner with almost absolute certainty. Thus, to share this piece of privacy requires a relationship of trust and security between the individual owner of the trait and the biometric system itself.

The biometric transaction is composed of human and machine. The human provides the raw data and, in turn, trusts the machine to safeguard it and use it for the intended purpose. For this sharing of privacy to continue and the trust to remain, all aspects of this transaction must be secured and the confidence kept by both parties.

Securing and Trusting a Biometric Transaction

The security and trust of a biometric transaction must begin at the presentation of the live biometric trait and continue through the final algorithm decision. This transaction path is made up of the following components:

- User
- Biometric reader
- Matching location

Each item that is part of the biometric transaction needs to be secured. Let's examine the transaction path in more detail.

User

The user is the starting point of any biometric transaction. If the biometric device being used is active, the user initiates a transaction by presenting his/her biometric trait. If the biometric device being used is passive, the transaction could be started before the user is aware of its presence. In both cases, the user needs to have situational awareness about himself/herself and the environment. If the user is in an environment that is using passive biometrics, then the user has little control over when the transaction begins. Therefore, the user needs to know that a passive biometric is being used and to be prepared for a transaction taking place once the user is in range of the passive device. A passive transaction, for example, could be the authorization of opening a door, passing a security checkpoint, registering for time and attendance, network authentication, or public security surveillance. If the environment uses active biometric devices, then the user can decide when the transaction takes place. An active transaction, for example, could be door access, logical computer access, or access to time and attendance applications. In an active biometric environment, the user needs to submit to the measurement. The use of active biometrics is pro-privacy and allows the user to better safeguard his/her biometric data.

As mentioned, a user can secure the beginning of a biometric transaction by having situational awareness. Situational awareness allows the user to safeguard the use of his/her biometric data. The trust of the user, however, begins at the time of enrollment. When the user enrolls in a biometric system, a moment of trust happens. The user willingly presents himself/herself for enrollment. Before enrollment happens, the physical identity of a user is often verified by some other method. This verification is usually made by a government-issued identification, by an employer-issued identification, or by another trusted authority vouching for the user's identity. What happens is that this moment of trust becomes predicated on a previous moment of trust. That is, we must believe that the government-issued identification or the employer-issued identification is valid. The credibility of the trusted authority vouching for the user needs to be trusted as well. This results in another tradeoff. If the biometric measurement is based on a previous moment of trust, then it is in the best interest of everyone concerned to choose the most reliable moment of trust. It is quite feasible that, based on what the biometric transaction is to authorize or secure, multiple previous moments of trust may need to be verified. Thus, as with biometric technology, a risk level needs to be defined. If the strength of the previous moment of trust is great enough, this then becomes an acceptable risk.

Biometric Reader

The biometric reader is the interaction point of the user with the biometric system. The reader will take the physical trait and digitize it into raw biometric data. The raw biometric data is then transformed into a template for comparison. The location where the transformation and comparison take place depends on the biometric system. The mechanics of the biometric system can affect the trust and security of the biometric transaction.

Biometric readers fall into one of two categories:

- Trusted biometric devices
- Non-trusted biometric devices

Trusted biometric devices

Trusted biometric devices make comparison decisions that are assumed to be uncompromised. That is, the capture, templating, and comparison occurs on the same physical device. It does not communicate with the host computer for any biometric function. It will provide a yes/no response to a request for authentication or, when used in conjunction with a storage token like a smart card or on-board cryptographic module, it will supply access to requested information. Unlike a workstation, a trusted device is a single-task device, that is, it is has pre-programmed functionality. As such, it does not require the general input and output connections that a general-purpose device requires. Since additional input/output are not required, it is very unlikely that the pre-programmed nature of the device can be changed. This gives it the ability to be trusted. By contrast, a workstation is not a trusted device. It is general-purpose and has many means of input/output. Malicious programs can be introduced to alter how it behaves and computes, that is, malicious software can be introduced that causes biometric comparisons to always match or never match. With a trusted device, this cannot occur.

The trustworthiness of a device is based on its pre-programmed state. A trusted device needs to be protected from malicious attacks in order to remain trusted. To accomplish this, the device needs to be hardened both physically and electronically.

Physical hardening[1]

To protect the integrity of a trusted device, access to the electronics needs to be protected. If a device is breached, it can no longer be trusted. To prevent this from happening, the following precautions need to be considered:

Make attempts at physical intrusion obvious–The electronics that control a trusted device are found inside the device. To reach these components, the external casing needs to be breached. Any attack on the case should leave evidence of the attempt. The material used in the casing should show scratches or pry marks from any attempted entry. The casing should be closed with methods that make it difficult to re-open, Also, the casing should use closing mechanisms that once re-opened, are broken.

Making attempts at entry obvious will provide the user or security manager with an indication of tampering. When a device seems to be compromised, it can be removed from use and evaluated.

Make internal tampering externally visible–If the external casing can be breached and the internal electronics reached, it is possible that external tampering will not be noticed. To add extra security to the trustfulness of a device, manufacturers can include some external manifestation of any internal intrusion. This external manifestation could take the form of changing the color of a tamper window, zeroing the EEPROMs (electrically erasable programmable read-only memory), or tripping a "dead-man's switch." Such an additional security mechanism should increase the complexity of a physical security breach.

Encapsulate internal components in epoxy–If the external casing is breached, the ease of access to the internal components should be minimized. The majority of the devices produced are not field-serviceable and therefore do not have a need for component access for replacement or troubleshooting. The encapsulation of components in epoxy is one more layer of defense against internal tampering. The intruder now needs to take the time to carefully remove the

---

1. Kingpin, "Attacks on and Countermeasures for USB Hardware Token Devices" (196 Broadway, Cambridge, MA), 2002, pp. 1–23.

epoxy. This can be a near-impossible feat. The epoxy used for encapsulation can withstand several thousand pounds of pressure per square inch and is normally cured using heat. Thus, prying and using heat will probably destroy the components or render the device inoperable.

Use glue with a high melting point–The more difficult an intrusion can be made, the less likelihood of success. As the difficulty increases, the resources required to be successful also increase. Using a glue with a high melting point increases the time, money, and resources required to be successful. The goal is to have a melting point that is high enough to either cause damage to the surrounding housing and components, or render the device inoperable.

Obscure part numbers–Any breach of security begins with reconnaissance and information-gathering. The more information that can be gained about a potential target before an attack is launched, the better the chances of its being successful. Therefore, the amount of information provided about a device should be limited to marketing requirements and general device identification. To that end, all reference numbers or markers should be removed. This could be done through etching or just sanding the component. If the components need to be identified, a secure design reference could be kept by the design department.

Restrict access to the EEPROMs–While it seems obvious to restrict access to the EEPROMs, they are quite often left exposed. The reasons for the exposure could be lack of experience, lack of funding for a new board layout, or a limited production run, where an EEPROM may be flashed with the latest firmware before release. The EEPROMs are a vital piece of the electronics. It is here that cryptographic or secret data may be stored, and if the firmware is flashable, it is kept in an EEPROM. Due to the nature of the information contained in this component, it needs the same level of protection as any other piece of circuitry.

Access to the EEPROMs can be restricted in the same way as access to other electronics. The use of epoxy encapsulation, obfuscation of part numbers, and the use of more secure chip mounting can help protect the EEPROMs.

Remove or inactivate future expansion points–As with the EEPROMs, it seems obvious to inactivate or remove unneeded access points and future expansion points. Again, for the same reasons that the EEPROMs are not protected, expansion points or unneeded access points are usually forgotten. Leaving these expansion points exposed could lead to the compromise of otherwise well-protected electronics. For example, in Kingpin's analysis of USB cryptographic tokens, a newer version of a token protected access to the EEPROM with epoxy encapsulation, yet future expansion traces allowed access to the EEPROMs.[2] This example makes it clear that if time and effort are put into securing certain components, leaving other means of access defeats the best intentions of the designer.

Reduce Electro-Magnetic Frequency (EMF) emissions– As stated earlier, reconnaissance is a large part of planning an attack. If an attacker can gain information from simple, non-intrusive means, this makes the job of compromising a system much easier. Monitoring EMF emissions does not require very sophisticated equipment. The information gained from EMF emissions may seem trivial and expensive to negate relative to their risk. The current attack methodologies use an experimental approach. For example, timing attacks work by measuring the timing characteristics of responses or signal latencies relative to a given PIN. The longer the latency, the closer the guessed PIN is to the actual PIN. These types of experimental attacks could use EMF emissions to gather this type of information. Thus, reducing EMF emissions makes an attacker's job more difficult.

Use good board layout and system design–To help secure a trusted device, the board and components placed on it can be designed to enhance security. The difficulty of following board traces increases if they are spread out over layers and if the data, power, and ground lines are alternated.[3] In addition, with the current trend of manufacturers providing systems on chip solutions, the number of external interfaces has greatly decreased. Spending some time thinking about vulnerabilities after the board design is complete could avert a potential disaster in the future.

Electronic hardening

A trusted device does the biometric templating and matching on the device itself. Since the decision-making is done on the device, physical and electrical hardening is very important. For electronic hardening of a trusted device, the following must be considered:

Protection of the flashable firmware–With the advent of the USB communication protocol for external peripherals, the use of

2. Kingpin, "Attacks on and Countermeasures for USB Hardware Token Devices" (196 Broadway, Cambridge, MA),2002, pp. 17–18.
3. *Ibid.*

flashable firmware has greatly increased. Flashable firmware allows a developer to make changes and upgrades to a device without replacing the internal integrated circuits. While this is a great feature for the customer and good for the developer, it can be an entry point for attacks. If the updating of the firmware is not strongly protected, malicious firmware code could be used to compromise the device. To protect the firmware, the following precautions should be taken.[4]

- Firmware should be encrypted and decrypted by the trusted device before updating.
- The updated firmware needs to be digitally signed. Before the update, the device verifies the signed firmware. The trusted device needs to get new public keys for verification and encryption from a trusted site.
- The firmware should be compiler-optimized before being released, and all debug and symbol information should be removed.

Integrity of communications to the host–Even a trusted device needs to communicate with its host. This communication could be a request for authentication by the host and a response to the request from the trusted device. It could be the sending of new firmware to the device, or the storage of information to a smart card or an on-board cryptographic module. This link will normally take the form of a USB connection. As such, some basic data security can be implemented to increase the overall security of the trusted device. The use of encryption for the data being transmitted and authentication while creating the link will increase the security of the device.

With the increased focus on security and breaking existing security methods, it makes sense to use the strongest possible solution available. To adequately protect the link between the host and a trusted device, the data should be encrypted before being sent. The data should also be signed and timestamped to prevent an attacker from recording a transaction and playing it back at a later time. To accomplish this, a shared secret is needed. A shared secret could be transmitted in the clear, but this could be intercepted by tapping the communication channel. The shared secret could be obfuscated in the host software and the firmware of the trusted device. The drawback to this is that the shared secret is in the software on the host and, given sufficient time, effort, and money,

---

4. Brian Oblivion and Kingpin, "Secure Hardware Design," Black Hat Briefings, July 26–27, 2000.

this shared secret could be compromised. And, once a shared secret is compromised, it is compromised for all systems.

A better approach is to use a Diffie-Hellman key exchange. A Diffie-Hellman key exchange allows both the device and the host to securely generate the same secret. In this configuration, both parties know a large prime number and another number referred to as the generator. Using the large prime and the generator, both parties compute a public number. Once the public number is generated, all the numbers can be exchanged. Once the exchange is done, both parties can generate the same secret.

One drawback to this is the possibility of an attacker sitting in the middle of the transaction. This attacker would be able to impersonate both ends of the transaction. That is, the attacker could compute his/ her own public number. When the host sends its public number to the device, the attacker could intercept it and send his/her public number to the device. When the device sends its public number to the host, the attacker once again could substitute his/her own number. Thus, when a transaction is to take place between the host and the device, the attacker can decrypt and re-encrypt for both parties using their own public numbers.

This happens because the device and the host have not authenticated each other. If the device and the host had authenticated each other, then they would know if they were talking to the right party. This securing of the Diffie-Hellman key exchange is referred to as a station-to-station protocol. To accomplish this, both the device and the host get a certificate from a trusted authority so that when either party receives data, it can verify the signature on the data as being legitimate. In this new configuration, an attacker can still intercept the exchange of the public keys, but the attacker is unable to trick the receiving party into accepting the re-encrypted data. The receiving party would verify the signature on the data to ensure it has not been tampered with.

When both parties use public keys and digital signatures for authenticating each other, additional cryptography can be applied. Either end of the transaction can use the other party's public key to encrypt the data being sent so that the attacker cannot even decrypt what is being sent. When the other party receives the data, that party decrypts it with the private key and verifies the signature and timestamp of the data.

With the addition of this electronic hardening, the trusted device is more reliable in its trust, and is proactively protecting itself and the data it provides.

Protection from external injections of spurious data– While a trusted device should be limited in the amount of I/O it provides, some will be necessary. These points of I/O can be used to attack a device by injecting spurious information into the system in an attempt to compromise the system itself or deny its use. Regardless of how the I/O of a device is used, some basic attacks should be taken into account. These include:

Buffer overflows–Any part of a trusted system that takes in information is generally buffering its received data. While the designer makes certain assumptions about the operation of a device, it may be possible to introduce data that would overflow the buffer. The buffer overflow could result in the innocuous consequence of a device hanging or being reset. In a severe situation, it could allow the execution of untrusted code. This can happen when data sent for input is formed in such a way that the first part of the data includes the untrusted code to be run and enough additional data to overflow the buffer. When the buffer overflows, the plan for the memory location of the next instruction to be executed is overwritten with the memory location of the untrusted code. When this occurs, the device is compromised and cannot be trusted.

Use of undocumented command sets and functionality– In many cases, when devices are being built and tested, developers will implement undocumented commands. These undocumented commands are normally used for troubleshooting or to create macro commands for frequently executed application programming interfaces (APIs). These undocumented command sets can allow an attacker to gain information from the device and possibly put the device into a testing mode. Many testing modes allow access to all memory and functions on the device. In this way, the attacker could change some stored data and then return the device to a normal operational mode.

An undocumented command set can also provide detailed debugging or line monitoring capabilities. For example, one early pioneering biometric device sometimes had an I/O device driver installed on the host machine, which allowed all the registers, stacks, and buffers to be communicated for debugging purposes.

These types of undocumented command sets and functionality need to be restricted with some sort of strong secret, or disabled altogether before the final shipment of firmware and integrated circuits are sent to production.

Improperly structured data elements–With the need for the trusted device to provide feedback or send data back to the host, some sort of I/O method needs to be used. This I/O method could include serial, parallel, USB, or wireless connectivity. All of these connectivity methods have well-defined and structured data communication models. In these models, the format, size, and timing of the data are described. Additionally, the model also describes any expected variation from the standards, which are also known as tolerances. These tolerances are normally taken into account during the design of the trusted device. Sometimes the design of a trusted device can push the bounds of the tolerances. When this happens, the device can become susceptible to improperly structured data elements. In these cases, the improperly structured data elements can have the same behavioral characteristics as a buffer overflow attack. An improperly structured data element could cause a device to fail or expose a new behavior not normally seen. If a device fails, it could fail in a state where it is now susceptible to probing, or it could respond with memory data that would not otherwise be made available.

A trusted system needs to guard against these types of attacks. If it fails from any of these types of attacks, it should fail in a closed state. That is, it should shut down or otherwise become inoperable. It is preferable to have a device unavailable to the user than to have confidential or private information exposed.

Changed data without physical contact[5]–It has long been known that spurious cosmic rays can cause stored information in computer memory or in transit on a bus to become corrupted. The use of ECC (error correcting code) memory does help in alleviating some of this concern, but large bit-level errors may go undetected by the ECC methods currently implemented. ECC memory is also an additional cost that many cost-sensitive industries do not want to incur. In addition, even with ECC memory, low-level data corruption could still occur on the memory or system bus, or in-process.

While it is possible to generate these types of cosmic rays here on Earth, the particular accelerators required would not be available to the average hacker. Other forms of radiation generation are available, but most are not powerful enough to have the desired effect. There are some radioactive materials used in the oil-drilling business that may generate the energy required, but they would be hard to acquire as well. One form of radiation that is always available to us, and is easy to control, is radiant heat. The use of radiant heat can cause a low-level mem-

---

5. Sudhakar Govindavajhala and Andrew W. Appel, "Using Memory Errors to Attack a Virtual Machine" (Dept. of Computer Science, Princeton University, Princeton, NJ), 2003.

ory error. These errors induced in memory have caused system crashes and losses of data. What if an attacker could induce these errors to his/her benefit?

A paper[6] published by Sudhakar Govindavajhala and Andrew W. Appel of Princeton University demonstrated in the Java machine framework that such bit errors could cause the execution of arbitrary code. While the paper explores these errors in the context of Java, it is not unreasonable to believe that the same methodology could be applied to other languages and memory/process security models. While many trusted devices are not written in Java, the supporting storage mechanisms for trusted devices may use Java as their operating system. This is of most concern to biometric vendors offering match on (smart) card (MOC). MOC works by storing the enrolled biometric in the smart card and implementing a biometric algorithm on the card for matching. Once the biometric is presented and templated, it is then processed on the card, and a match/no match is generated. Frequently, the smart card also stores cryptographic secrets or other confidential data. The match of the biometric is the release mechanism for that data. Thus, it may be possible to induce a bit-level error that causes the stored flag for match/no match to become flipped and allow access to the stored information. This new type of attack makes implementing active security measures more important.

As originally recommended by Kingpin in his research, the implementation of detectors for temperature and radiation is warranted. If an attack is detected, actions could be taken to avert the exposure of data. This could include the zeroing of any critical data, or the failure of a device in a closed state. The intrusion should also be recorded and made physically visible. While it may seem like science fiction, the reality is that fact has become fiction. We now have a method of using light/radiation and heat to attack computer systems.

Improper failure states–When systems are designed, much thought is given to how the system will function in its normal state, that is, when it is being used for the tasks for which it was intended. Some thought is put into error catching and maybe even error recovery. Little time and thought are currently given to the state in which the device will be left when it fails, however. If a device fails in such a way that it leaves itself open to change or probing, then it has lost its trustworthiness. At the same time, state machines are often used in the program-

---

6. *Ibid.*

ming of devices. These state machines need to have default error states that prevent the leak of confidential information if an exception happens, causing the state machine to crash. The default failure and error states must ensure that no system data can be retrieved or released.

Final thoughts on trusted devices

As seen from the previous discussion, a lot of effort and cost goes into making a trusted device. Companies that build trusted devices do so to sell them and turn a profit. This means that the costs of hardening will be passed on to the customer in the form of higher prices. What the customer needs to do is evaluate his/her risk model relative to the cost of the trusted device. If the risk analysis does not demonstrate a serious threat, then the use of a non-trusted device is warranted. If, on the other hand, the information or the activities that are to be biometrically protected have very serious consequences, then the additional cost of a trusted device can be justified.

Non-trusted biometric devices

A non-trusted biometric device is not able to make comparison decisions. Since the comparison decisions are taking place off the device, a certain amount of uncertainty is assumed to be present in the transaction. Since the device is not making the matching decision, that decision must occur somewhere else. This matching can take place on the connected host, on an authentication server, or on a smart card running an MOC algorithm. The choice of where the match is to take place is now also a case of risk mitigation. As we will see in the following discussion, the risk associated with each option does increase. The choice of where the match will occur should be based on the locations which the biometric system supports, and on the consequences of the transaction being compromised.

Matching Location

Matching can be done in one of four locations. The location where the templating occurs can be independent of where the matching takes place. The next sections will discuss where templating could take place for use with each of the following matching locations:

1. Trusted device
2. Local host

3. Authentication server

4. MOC (smart card)

Local Host

The local host is the interaction point of the biometric system with the software requesting biometric authentication. If a trusted device is used, then there is a secure link between the device and the local host. Also, as described earlier, it is ideal if both the local host and the trusted device have authenticated each other through the use of certificates. This assures the software running on the local system that the match/no match response from the trusted device is valid.

If the local host is not interacting with a trusted device, then the local host will need to exhibit one of two behaviors. If the local host is not doing the matching, then it must act as a secure conduit for the biometric information to reach an authentication server. If this is the case, then the local host may do the templating of the raw biometric data. This may involve the local host decrypting the raw data from the reader, templating the data, and re-encrypting the data for transmission and eventually comparison at the authentication server. This would mean that while templating is taking place, the raw biometric data and the template itself are exposed to possible interception and attack. To reduce the risk of the raw data or template being compromised, the templating could take place at the authentication server. If the templating does take place at the authentication server, this adds another level of activity for the server. If the server is intended to do high-volume matching, the templating of individual user data will only slow it down. Thus, templating often takes place on the local host. If templating must occur on the local host, then the following precautions should be taken:

- The templating and encrypt/decrypt operation should take place in a secure area of memory.
- All temporary buffers and variables should be cleared after use.
- The data should never be written to disk.
- The local workstation should be up-to-date with the latest operating system service packs and security patches.
- Anti-virus software should be run to prevent malicious code from being introduced on the system.

- The matching software should validate that its components have not been switched, or that its underlying resources have not been tampered with.
- If possible and supported by the host operating system, the matching should be done through statically linked applications. This prevents dependencies on underlying system components that could be compromised.

Even with the above precautions taken, there will always be some risk that the transaction will be compromised. The main reason for this is that most host systems are running untrusted operating systems. The local host is often the primary computing platform for the user, and as such, is constantly being updated with new software. This means that we cannot implicitly trust these platforms.

Matching on the local host is the last choice for matching a biometric template. In order of preference, is most secure, followed by a trusted device, a MOC, a match on the server, and finally, a match on the local host.

Authentication Server

The authentication server is generally a single-purpose server. It is used to verify the reference template to the stored template. In doing so, it provides services with biometrics similar to those network login servers provide for passwords. Thus, the authentication server needs to be protected in the same manner as a network login server. These servers are generally used in a secure room or facility with controlled access to the console. Secure access to the machine and the console is necessary in order to safeguard the integrity of the server. It is well-known that if an attacker can reach the server physically, it can in general be compromised. In addition to keeping the server physically secure, the same precautions that were taken for local host authentication are also applicable.

If the authentication server will also template the raw data, then the authentication device and the server should authenticate to each other with certificates. This way, the device knows that its raw data will arrive at the trusted authentication server, and the authentication server knows that it is talking directly to a device and not to a replay of a previous transaction. In addition, the local host now acts as a conduit for data. As such, the local host should not touch the transmitted data other than to assist in its forwarding to the authentication server.

If the local host will template the data, then the authentication server must secure the transactional link and support encryption of the data. The same methodologies that were outlined in the electronic hardening of a trusted device are also useful in securing the communications between the server and local host, or the device itself.

The authentication server needs to authenticate itself with the local host so that it can transmit the outcome of biometric data matching in a secure manner.

Matching on the server is preferred over local host matching. It is still more preferable to have a trusted device. If a trusted device is cost-prohibitive, then having a properly secured server is a powerful second option.

Match on Card (MOC)

As the name implies, biometric matching can take place on a smart card. While this appears to be an ideal solution, the implementation of the solution is very important. When considering MOC, the following questions need to be answered:

- Where does the template get created?
- What communication methods are used between the biometric device and smart card?
- How is the algorithm implemented on the card?

Where is the template created?

When the templating is done on the local host, this opens the transaction up to attack. If by using a MOC solution the actual templating takes place on the local host, then this is no better a solution than matching on the local host. Once the template is exposed to the PC bus, even with the precautions discussed in local host templating, an element of uncertainty has now been introduced into the transaction. MOC solutions may template on the local machine due to a lack of speed or system resources on the smart card. For an ideal solution, the card itself would do the biometric templating.

What communication methods are used between the biometric device and the smart card?

Regardless of where the template is created from the raw data, either the raw data or an externally created template needs to reach the smart card. This communication path needs to be as secure as possible. If this path involves exposure to the PC bus, then once again, an element of uncertainty is introduced into the transaction. If, on the other hand, the biometric data moves internally in the device, never leaves the device, and travels across secure buses, then this is a strong matching solution from a security standpoint.

How is the algorithm implemented on the card?

Many vendors, when trying to implement a MOC solution, take short-cuts with their algorithm to get acceptable performance from the matching. Any change to the algorithm invalidates the current biometric statistics. Therefore, it is important to have a vendor clearly state what its biometric statistics are for MOC.

Getting the performance increases that MOC providers are looking for can involve templating taking place elsewhere. When templating takes place off the card, the template can be compromised. Thus, a certain degree of uncertainty is introduced into the transaction. Another method of increasing performance is to have some binning and pre-comparison work for the match take place on a faster processor. This normally involves using the local host. As seen before, the same issues with using a matching location can affect this plan.

A vendor may also adjust its measurements of any algorithm's strength. When matching takes place in application software, algorithm strength may be greater. For example, the vendor may have biometric security levels of high, medium, and low for matching in application software. The vendor could say that the MOC has a high, medium, and low level of biometric security. Since the same vendor is claiming the same security levels regardless of where the matching takes place, the user might assume that the security settings are equivalent. As we have seen, this may not be the case, depending on whether the same algorithm is implemented in both locations in the same way.

Final thoughts on matching location

As in every other business decision that needs to be made, risk is a large deciding factor. If the risk of a compromised transaction is sufficiently strong, then the use of a trusted device is warranted. For most transactions and applications, the use of an authentication server will meet the users' needs appropriately. For much lower risk transactions, or if using biometrics purely for convenience, local host matching may be sufficient.

Conclusion

It is clear from examining the biometric transaction that privacy can be truly guaranteed only when adequate security measures are taken. The security measures must be in place from the time when the user is ready to authenticate to the moment when the matching decision is made.

The threats to a biometric transaction are numerous and always present. Therefore, continuous vigilance is necessary to keep the authentication and local hosts patched, and ensure that only the proper people are accessing the local host and authentication server, Even with the best security methods in place, there will still be some level of uncertainty in the transaction. That feeling of uncertainty will be directly proportional to the risk of the methods used during biometric transactions. Hopefully, an increase of time, money, and effort will sufficiently reduce the number of people able to attack a biometric system.

12

Preparing for the Proof of Concept and Selecting a Vendor

There are many different types of biometric systems available on the market. Chapter 4 explained what makes a good biometric for network security. Once the decision has been made about which biometric system to use, it needs to be implemented in the company. Since this particular implementation will impact the daily use of the network and the applications on the users' desktops, it cannot be done without planning and testing. The stages in accomplishing this include:

- Preparation for the proof of concept (POC) and vendor selection
- Pilot design and implementation
- Final deployment and rollout of the biometric system

Each of the above stages comprises a separate chapter in this section. Each stage is dependent on the success of the previous one, which means that every stage needs to be completed. Skipping stages will result in failures and disappointments in the biometric system.

Two examples will further illustrate the application of the methodologies being discussed. The examples are a culmination of actual implementations done over several years. The names and companies have been changed, but the situations are real. At the end of each example, the actual methodologies are explained in detail.

The first example is told from the perspective of Martin. Martin works for a Fortune 500 financial institution as a senior manager for a technology group. Martin's story illustrates what happens when the suggested methodologies are used.

The second example is told from the perspective of Jason. Jason works for a large corporate enterprise with locations throughout the world and is a project manager working for the corporate IT organization. Jason's story illustrates what happens when the suggested methodologies are not adhered to.

The POC and vendor selection involve the following steps:

1. Define the driver of the project as either corporate IT or a business need
2. Define the business need or objectives
3. Designate the internal sponsor of the project
4. Define the stakeholders
5. Define a clear set of goals and success criteria for the project
6. Form and charter the POC group
7. Based on the goals and success criteria, invite a few vendors to pilot
8. Set the timelines for the POC and ensure that the implementation activities are done within the scope of the POC
9. Deploy the POC
10. Monitor and evaluate the POC
11. Wrap up the POC
12. Decide on the validity of each vendor's solution
13. Make a go/no go decision to move ahead
14. Announce the results and lay the groundwork for the next phase

Each part of the POC is discussed in great detail in this chapter.

Define the Driver of the Project as Either Corporate IT or a Business Need

Martin hated Mondays. On Mondays, his limited technical support staff spent most of the time resetting passwords for traders. Martin looked after the technology needs of a global trading group for his company. The traders were there for one reason: to generate money. They were not concerned with remembering passwords, or knowing that each others' passwords was a security risk. They just wanted to make money. Thus, every Monday—and even worse if it was a Tuesday after a long weekend—the traders would flood the floor, and immediately Martin's help desk would get overwhelmed with requests for password resets. He also knew that by this time, the head trader of each group had picked a new password for the week, one that all the other traders were told to use. This way, any trader in a group could cover the position of another if someone was away from a trading station. This gave Martin no end of grief. He was tired of this self-defeating cycle and wanted to find a better approach. The real fly in the ointment was the password itself. Traders had passwords for everything! A typical trader would have 12–15 passwords per day to use. In addition, the password rules among applications were inconsistent and thus prevented the use of the same passwords. Martin realized that if he could replace the password with something more easily remembered, he could maybe alleviate, if not eliminate, the password reset deluge every Monday. Martin had recently attended a trade show at which he had seen a company that sold fingerprint biometric devices which also had the ability to replace the Windows login. This seemed like a good starting point. If he could get biometrics in place on the trading floor, surely the traders could remember to bring their fingers to work. Thus, his mission was clear: His business unit would need to drive a biometrics project for password replacement.

Jason looked over the latest project reports for the deployment of digital certificates for email signing. They showed that the project was moving ahead, but with some red flags. The project had been initiated because someone had sent a spoofed email purporting to have come from the CEO to all employees promising large pay raises. This email was too good to be true, as it had been faked. This incident clearly showed the weakness of unsigned and encrypted emails. The company had spent millions in organizing a digital signature outsourcing arrangement. The company had procured licenses for all the employees and, after going through training, each employee was to be issued a digital certificate. The project up to this point had gone very smoothly, but a new wrinkle was just thrown into the plans. The security group had sent out an unsolicited email to senior management, red-flagging the project for lax security. It seemed that one of their security engineers had attended a training session and had found out that the passwords being used were relatively weak so that users could remember them, and that the digital certificates themselves were being stored on local hard disks. These two things made the security group believe that an easy attack could get the digital certificate and compromise the password, leading to faked but signed email messages. This left Jason with a project that had high visibility and was currently under scrutiny for security concerns. He had suggested stronger passwords, but the user community had rebelled. He proposed storing the certificates on smart cards, but again, the security group said that protecting them with weak passwords was still no good. Jason now needed to provide a way to deliver digital certificates to the company and satisfy the security group. Jason finally hit on the solution: Use a biometric to replace the password and, ideally, have that biometric work with smart cards as well. He would tie in this new biometric project with the support of the digital certificate project and, in this way, avoid the meddling of the security group in this new initiative. After all, he had satisfied their original objection to weak passwords. He would replace them with a biometric. Besides, he was from the corporate IT group, which had a mandate to deliver new technologies to the company. He was in the perfect position to drive this project forward.

The Methodology

The origination of a project can affect how the project is managed and put together. It can also clearly define what group in the company should lead the effort. If the project is being driven by regulations or risk management, it can succeed in being driven by IT as long as the IT group can find a lead business unit. This lead business unit should be the one being regulated or risk-managed. Additionally, IT needs to have a global vision that the project will likely be rolled out to the rest of the company.

Jason clearly has the mandate to deliver his biometric project. There is a risk to be managed, and it is clear that the current status quo is not acceptable. He has not yet defined a lead business unit. This could be difficult to do, as the digital signature project is company-wide. Biometrics for Jason need to be implemented as a way to increase security.

If the project is being driven by a business unit, it needs to have clear goals, objectives, and buy-in from the employees of the business unit. The business unit driving the project must involve IT from the earliest steps to increase the chances of success. Even if the business unit is a profit center, it is still dependent on the IT staff for support. It is better to have everyone informed and involved than to try to force something through that one of the partners may not want.

Martin definitely has the right idea. He is supporting a business unit that is a profit center, and his goals are clear. Biometrics will be used to replace passwords, and they will be positioned to increase user convenience. Martin realizes that biometrics can also increase security, but in selling the technology this way, he will need to provide a much stronger level of proof of their accuracy.

Define the Business Need or Objectives

Martin was starting to put his project together. The project objectives would involve the use of biometrics to reduce user inconvenience and, at the same time, help with the risk management of shared passwords. Both objectives were hot buttons for management. Management wanted the traders to be as productive as possible and also, if possible, they wanted to reduce the risks of conducting business. Martin felt confident in his objectives.

Jason looked at what was facing him. He had a promising global project that could possibly be delayed or scrapped because of the concerns of the security group. Jason needed biometrics to strongly secure the users' digital certificates and silence the concerns of the security group.

The Methodology

For the successful overall deployment of a biometric solution, there must be a driving business need or objective. Without this, it will be difficult to set performance goals and objectives, money spent on the project will be tough to justify, and finding an internal sponsor will be next to impossible. Some of the main business needs or objectives should include:

- Regulatory–The regulating bodies of the company's industry may have put into place regulatory requirements for the use of strong authentication. The regulatory bodies may have created requirements for the removal of shared credentials. To conduct e-commerce activities in the industry, a strong binding needs to be provided between the employees of the company and their electronic representation.

- Risk management–The company's own risk management group may drive the adoption of the biometric system. The members should be looking at ways to reduce the internal risk for weak passwords or the sharing of passwords. They may also see biometrics as a way to increase security.

- User inconvenience–The help desk managers and business unit IT support group are constantly besieged with the users' need to reset passwords. As more applications come to the users' desktops, the majority of them have their own password authentication mechanisms. Thus, a new application on the desktop means a new password to remember. This large number of passwords is a source of inconvenience and it is also a security risk. By implementing SSO in conjunction with a biometric system, user inconvenience is reduced, and system security is maintained or improved.

- Introduction of PKI–With the move to doing more business over the Web, the need to authenticate and validate transactions and individuals is increasingly difficult to meet. The use of a digital certificate in combination with a digital signature is very useful. If digital signatures are to be used for transactions in which non-repudiation is desirable, protecting access to the certificate with only a password seems weak. The implementation of a biometric to provide a strong physical binding of an individual to his/her certificate provides true non-repudiation, removes one more password that needs to be remembered, and increases the overall security of the solution.

- Better password management–This business driver goes hand in hand with user convenience. If we can find a better solution to password management and reduce password resets, all parts of the company benefit. The user benefits from increased convenience, the IT group benefits from reduced calls to the help desk and the assignment of staff to higher-value functions, and the company benefits because the cost of doing business decreases and risk management is satisfied.

Once the business driver is identified, a lead business unit needs to be defined. The success of the project increases if that business unit is a profit center. Profit centers normally have the ears of the CEO and CFO. These two company managers can make or break a project. If the project is seen as expensive, the fact that a profit center is leading the way increases the likelihood of the project's survival. Since the profit center makes money, anything that makes its job easier or increases its morale is good for the company. Once you have your lead business unit, identifying an executive sponsor becomes easier.

Designate the Internal Sponsor of the Project

Martin had worked for the company a long time. He had seen many projects come and go. He knew that the successful ones always had a strong executive leading the charge. Martin himself was not exactly a political lightweight in his senior management position, but it never hurt to have someone else share the burden of sponsorship. Martin knew the man he wanted was John, who had been with the company for almost 15 years and had survived many mergers and projects. John was the head of the IT group for Martin's business unit. He knew that his senior management would support John's projects because John consistently delivered; also, the head traders he supported were always ready to mention in conversation to senior management how important John's projects were to their work.

Jason had been in a project manager's role for only a short time. He had risen through the ranks of his company quickly, carried along by the pull of his manager. Because his manager was a star in the organization, he was able to bring his people along with him as he was promoted. Jason was seen by some as a hanger-on, getting his position only because of whom he knew. Jason resented that and worked hard. Sometimes his hard work left him deaf to valuable feedback from others. Quite often, this feedback was not always tactful. Jason knew that his senior manager would support his project, but the latter's tolerance for problems was decreasing. After the blindside the security group had provided, a little of the glow on his name had fallen off. Jason needed this project to go smoothly.

The Methodology

Now that we have identified the lead business unit, the internal sponsor will probably come from this group. The internal sponsor should be a mid- to senior-level manager, and not necessarily an executive. The mid- to senior-level manager is normally in a good place in the company management chain to have interactions with both workers in the business unit and the senior executive responsible for the business unit. By having a foot in each camp, the sponsor can act as a point of contact for the project and can direct the flow of information. If the sponsor hears that senior management may want to reduce or eliminate the project, the sponsor can gather positive feedback to pass on to the senior executive, or can give the project a heads-up of what is to come. Mid- to senior-level managers, who are normally in the thick of the political ebb and flow of the company, are usually able to direct resources and give advice that can help the project. They may even redirect subversive actions. Awareness of the subversive undercurrents that surround a project can help the project thrive and continue. In addition, when internal group conflicts arise during the pilot, the sponsor can help smooth ruffled feathers or grease the rails to make the tough work easier.

In accepting this role, the sponsor needs to be prepared to dedicate significant time to the project. If the sponsor is there to be merely a figurehead or gloryhound, the project can be at risk due to a lack of attention. At the same time, the sponsor needs to allow the project his/her room to grow and mature. Micromanaging may introduce conflict and slow consensus-building.

Define the Stakeholders

Martin had previously experienced the problems that can arise if all parties are not consulted when an important project is undertaken. Involving the internal parties responsible for the different areas of technology that the project would touch could prevent possible backlash later. This way, it would be impossible for any group to stand up and stop the project by saying it was not involved. Martin knew that the number of possible stakeholders could be large, so he delegated the management of certain stakeholders to others in his organization. This way, he could cover all possible bases. Martin knew most of the senior management personally. He knew which ones were technology-friendly and which were not. Martin knew of one particular senior executive who loved new technology. The more leading-edge the technology, the more he liked it. This senior executive was viewed by his peers as the gatekeeper for new technology. If he liked it, they rubber-stamped the corporate decision on the technology. If he panned the new technology, they would not even discuss the technology project.

Jason knew time was short. The deadline for the certificate project was quickly approaching, as was any funding that was available for the biometric project. Jason needed for the biometrics pilot to move ahead as quickly as possible. He felt that since he was part of the corporate IT, he really did not need to involve that many people. He could get his sponsor to apply pressure to the managers to get what he needed from the different groups. This way, he could avoid having a large group of stakeholders to manage.

To ensure success in a project, the selection of stakeholders is important. The stakeholders represent all the interested parties in the project. The stakeholders should be drawn from the following areas:

- Help desk–This group will need to support what is deployed. Once the project moves from POC to pilot and then to deployment, the help desk will be the first line of support. Help desk people in general are already overworked, and under-appreciated, and the introduction of a new system into the mix can increase their anxiety. It is always easier for them to blame the newest piece of software installed on a system as the cause of a problem rather than troubleshoot the issue. If, on the other hand, the help desk feels included in the project and has its concerns voiced, the pilot and deployment have a greater chance of success.

- Desktop engineering–This group manages the desktop build and the software that is deployed. Like the help desk, this group is in a constant battle to maintain what is in place. This group is also under pressure to deploy new solutions. Therefore, the group will be skeptical of anything that is going to change the desktop builds. In many organizations, it can take 6–9 months to get a new piece of software accepted for deployment. If the desktop engineering group has a project forced on it without any input or involvement, the chances for a successful project are zero!

- Server engineering–This group manages the servers and back-end systems used for authentication. Depending on how the biometric system works, the project may need to use some server resources. Whether those resources are used for authentication or data storage, the project is interacting with managed resources. The server engineering group may need to make special modifications to the security structure running on those servers, or apply specific patches that the biometric system requires. In either event, the inclusion of the server engineering team will allow the group to have full knowledge of what is being done. It also allows the project to get valuable feedback from the server engineering group on lead times to get certain tasks completed.

- Risk management–This group has the responsibility of managing and defining the acceptable risks and mitigation procedures for the company. Since the biometric system will interact with authentication mechanisms, and may require other risk management polices to be set aside so the project can proceed, the group is an invaluable part of the stakeholder group. This group will see the driving business needs of the project. The team can also voice concerns over activities planned, or make the project team aware of risk management directives that need to be followed. Including this group at the beginning of the process makes future conflicts with risk management guidelines easier to solve. This way, the risk management team cannot say it was unaware of what was going on since the group was part of the project from the start.

- IT security–This group engineers and evaluates the security infrastructure of the network. Since the biometric system may interface into other systems or, in some cases, replace what already exists, the IT security team's early buy-in and acceptance are critical. IT security workers tend to be the best and brightest, and they often have preconceived notions of what will and will not work. In particular, the need to overcome the "not invented here" mentality is crucial. If this group is not brought into the project early on and given a chance to vet the solution numerous times, the project will die a slow and lingering death! IT security members can work with others if a mutual partnership is established based on trust and compromise. There are issues on which the project team will need the IT group to compromise, and on others, the compromise will have to be made by the project team.

- Business unit representation—The business unit is the customer for the project. It is this group's requirements that must be met. The group is there to provide feedback directly to the project from the end-users. It should have a strong voice in the project. There is no use delivering a biometric system that the end-users will not use. Thus, the satisfaction of the business unit is very important.

- A strong and politically savvy executive—This person will know the lay of the political landscape and can help direct and divert efforts, both helpful and harmful. This executive will work in conjunction with the project sponsor. The project sponsor will be the day-to-day interface between the executive stakeholders and the project team. The executive as a stakeholder will represent the project in the executive circles and be responsible for the financial and overall project deliverables.

Define a Clear Set of Goals and Success Criteria for the Project

Martin understood the frustration of his users. He too had many of the same applications that the traders used. All employees of the company had to log in to both a Windows domain and a Novell directory. To access Internet-based applications and financial provider Web sites, each user needed to enter a user ID and password for login to the firewall and proxy. Also, the mail system had a different password and most of the trading systems were Windows-based. To evaluate the reduction in password resets, Martin examined his help desk log and found that the majority involved the login to the network, then to mail, then to the Web, and lastly, to the trading applications. Martin then defined his success criteria for password reductions as being able to log into the network, mail, the Web, and two trading applications. If this could be accomplished, he felt that it could be sold to senior management for piloting and eventually deployment. The company had experimented with biometrics previously. The experience had not been overly positive because many users could not use the biometric on a day-to-day basis. It was also found that many employees could not even be enrolled in the system. Martin believed that for a biometric system to be deployed, 90–95% of the user population needed to accept this technology. The biometric system also needed to enroll 95–97% of its user population.

Jason needed to show that biometrics could work to protect the users' digital certificates. It was that simple.

The Methodology

Based on the objectives that were defined earlier in the process, clear goals and success criteria in obtaining the goals should be defined. The goals should be milestoned and built on previous wins; they should not take large leaps in technology or project scale. The success criteria are defined so that in striving to be successful, the goals are met. The success criteria are what the different phases of the project will be measured against when they are completed. This will be used to make a go/no go decision. Where possible, the success criteria should be objective and well-defined. For example, a success criterion stating that the end-users must accept the technology is subjective. A success criterion which states that the end-users should show a greater than 95% willingness to continue with the project based on a standard survey is a measurable objective. In addition, it is important to set early expectations of what error rates are acceptable for the project. Setting success criteria supports the goal of having a deployable and usable biometric system. To assign values to these success criteria, the chosen vendor needs to provide some guidance. Usually, the vendor will provide a more positive range of values than what will actually be seen. Knowing this ahead of time will allow the project team to set reasonable expectations.

Goals come in two forms. The first is a goal for a completion date or use of a feature. As a project progresses through its various phases, these goals will need to be evaluated and adjusted. The second: the whole point of doing a POC, piloting, and then deploying is to have reasonable goals and expectations for the project by the time it is deployed. The goals will also guide the project as it progresses. Adjusting a goal does not imply a missed requirement, but rather a growing and maturing with the technology.

Form and Charter the POC Group

Martin brought his project team and stakeholders together. He outlined what was to be done and how it was to be accomplished. The project would deliver on the network login, mail, Web, and only two trading applications. The POC would be deployed only on existing infrastructure and to only one branch of the trading community. All the technology stakeholders would have two representatives involved with the POC. Martin and his immediate team would make the vendor selection based on the goals and success criteria.

Jason met with his manager to review what was to take place. Jason had arranged for some colleagues in the project management office to be part of the POC. It seemed a reasonable choice, as these were the same people who were part of the digital certificate POC. They really didn't mind the password, but would be glad to try out a new technology. Jason's manager informed him that during a senior management meeting, the topic of passwords had come up. It seemed that there was growing user concern over having to remember passwords. In the discussion that followed, it seemed logical that Jason's current biometric replacement for a digital certificate password could be extended to other applications. His manager thought this would a good idea and felt that it should not entail any additional cost. Jason would need to find a biometric system that could replace digital certificate passwords as well as other Windows-based passwords. The same colleagues he had selected earlier would still work, as they had Windows logins. So, the charter was changed to include other Windows-based passwords.

The Methodology

Once all the stakeholders have been identified and invited into the project, and the goals and success criteria for the project have been defined, the POC charter should be created. The charter will define what percentage or part of the overall project goal will be used in the POC, and what other short-term POC goals should be defined. The scope of the POC is defined and agreed to. When setting goals and deciding on scope, the following can help in achieving POC success:

- Remember that less is quite often better—When looking at the possible high values that the project can deliver, it is easy to want to increase the scope or be more aggressive in the feature set of the products being considered. It is better to follow the "keep it simple" rule early on, and expand later during the pilot.

- Leverage existing infrastructures–When trying to get financial approval for a project, it is better to show the highest possible value from the project with the lowest possible cost. To do this, it is advisable to leverage existing infrastructure. Doing this has some benefits. The first benefit is that the infrastructure is already deployed and being managed. This means that there is no cost to the POC group, and the time that would be required to deploy the infrastructure can be used to do other tasks. Another benefit is that the POC, if not successful, will leave orphaned infrastructure behind to be decommissioned.
- Hit high-value objectives and goals first–It is always better to grab the low-hanging fruit first than to go after the brass ring on the first attempt. By doing this, the overall project will scale up through all its phases.
- Integrate the application that everyone uses, not the orphaned one from three mergers ago!–If part of the POC is using the biometric system with existing applications, it is best to integrate the application that will be used by the most members of the POC user base. By doing this, the maximum number of users in the group will be using the biometric system the maximum amount of time. This will help generate the feedback that is needed for making decisions at the end of the POC. It will also provide the greatest test of the biometric system.
- Be less aggressive; don't push the full feature set–This will allow for a greater probability of success for the POC. The POC needs to prove only that the technology is applicable enough to move on to the pilot phase. In the later stages of the project, more parts of the product's feature set can be used.
- Build some wins and momentum before venturing into riskier actions–This goes hand in hand with not pushing the feature set. If the feature set is reduced, wins and momentum can be built quickly. It is better to walk slowly from the starting line than to leave quickly and trip on your shoelaces!
- Make sure all the groups are equally involved–It is amazing that in a professional corporate environment, professionals can behave like young children. If one group is feeling neglected or another group is receiving favored attention, this will cause dissension in the project. It is easy to forget that there are other

stakeholders for the POC aside from the lead business unit. The other members of the group need to be using the biometric system as well. This is how they will build confidence in the system and provide meaningful feedback. It is better to get feedback from each group as early as possible. If it is negative, it can be dealt with and the POC can be adjusted, or proposed changes can be put forward for the next phases.

When the charter is defined, all parties need to sign off on it, including the executive sponsor. This is the recognition that there has been consensus and all parties are ready to move forward.

Based on the Goals and Success Criteria, Invite a Few Vendors to Pilot

Based on his requirements and well-padded timelines, Martin had a large field of possible vendors, which he eventually narrowed down to three. All three fit the charter well and could provide initial support for the POC. All three were relatively young companies in an emerging biometric marketplace. Martin figured the winner of the POC would be the company that performed better than the others when their technology failed.

Jason had a curve thrown at him. The additional requirement of replacing other passwords with a biometric was not expected. This now left Jason with a requirement for a biometric system that could both support digital certificates and replace Windows-based passwords. The choice of vendors was limited and, with the digital certificate deadline approaching, time was not a luxury he could afford. Jason needed to do a quick POC. He would have the vendors focus on the digital signatures and, if time permitted, test Windows passwords support.

The Methodology

If the charter of the POC group is clear, the number of vendors to consider should be greatly reduced. In a corporate environment, every biometric system vendor wants that next sale. To that end, the vendors will lobby for a chance to be a part of the POC. The vendor selection needs to be based on:

- The vendor's applicability to the charter—This will normally be revealed when the charter is turned into a Request for Proposal, and after an examination of the vendors' responses. From these responses, the most promising vendors will be selected and invited to make oral presentations. The vendor that best articulates the ability to meet the charter and demonstrates knowledge of your company and industry should be considered.

- The vendor's ability to provide detailed support during all phases of the project–Many companies are running lean and have employees doing multiple duties, in which case, a former vendor employee may not always be available. At the same time, as a potential customer, a company which pays for some consulting support or purchases a support plan shows that the enterprise is serious about the POC. Since this is a POC, it is proper to expect that a number of issues will be identified, and a level of commitment should be made by the vendor to support the company in its POC.

- The vendor's financial viability–While the POC is for a limited period of time, the usable life of the biometric system may be in the three- to five-year timeframe. As was seen by the dot-com bust of a few years ago, long-term financial stability is important. For vendors that are public, it is easy to see what their financial viability is and what debt rating they carry. On the other hand, private or start-up companies may not have the same level of transparency as a public vendor. Therefore, it is important to vet their financial position as much as possible.

- Previous work done in the same industry–While there are many similarities among industries, experience specific to your company's industry is always preferable. For example, the financial vertical will have different challenges and requirements than the healthcare industry. Having done work for other companies in the industry vertical, the project team can learn from the previous experiences of the selected vendor.

- High completion rate on sales–Vendors will always be more than willing to talk about the sales they have made. What they do not offer freely is their completion rate. For example, early on in the biometric industry, one industry player claimed to have shipped tens to hundreds of thousands of units. When further investigation was done, it was found that the shipped units were sitting in a warehouse collecting dust. It is one thing to be able to sell a product, it is quite another to get it deployed. If the vendor tends to have lots of sales with a low deployment rate, then further due diligence is required. On the other hand, a high completion rate is a good indication of the quality of the biometric system its vendor.

- Willingness to work as part of the team–Lately, there has been a recognition by both the vendor and the customer of the need to work together as part of the project team. The project team needs to be willing to accommodate the vendor in its groups and activities. Conversely, the vendor needs to provide dedicated resources in order to pull its weight as part of the team.

Using the above suggestions, vendors should be selected quickly, and expectations of the vendor's participation need to be set for both the vendor and the project team. Vendors who did not make the cut need to be thanked for their time and informed of not being selected. Such courtesy extended by the company should enable it to hire the vendors for possible future solutions, and it allows the vendors to move on to their next opportunity.

Set the Timelines for the POC and Ensure That the Implementation Activities Are Done Within the Scope of the POC

Martin and his team had decided to let the vendors have 5 days to set up their infrastructure and get 10 POC members deployed. Once the POC was deployed, the members would then run the solution for 2 weeks. The vendors' solutions would run in parallel on different members' machines in each represented technology group.

Jason looked at the calendar and sighed. The deadline for digital certificates was quickly approaching. If he was to make his deadline, he would need to limit the POC. Jason had previously selected a vendor and asked the vendor to install a team in 2 days. Subsequent to that, the POC would last 10 days.

The Methodology

When deciding how long to run a POC, there is a general feeling that longer is better. The timeframe needs to be long enough to validate the technology, but not so long as to have the POC stagnate. Generally, 30–45 days is long enough to know if the technology being proposed will meet the success criteria of the project. By keeping it short, the following benefits can be seen:

- Keeps the POC focused—By keeping the POC limited in its timeframe, the POC team must focus on the goals and success criteria. Letting the POC run on will tend to encourage experimentation. The members of the pilot become bored with what has been accomplished and may start trying things that are not yet ready to use. If this causes failures, the failures may be incorrectly interpreted by others outside the project as failures of the POC.
- Builds on momentum—If the POC is successful, there will be excitement and momentum created. This in turn will create energy and drive, which can then be leveraged to kick-start the pilot phase of the project.

If the POC is failing, keeping it short allows the failure to be completed quickly and then used as a learning tool. Since there will not be the frustration felt from using a product that does not meet the company's needs, additional vendor products can be brought in for evaluation.

Deploy the POC

Martin was so looking forward to the POC. He had involved all the stakeholders equally. He had insured that the traders taking part in the POC had a backup machine in case something unexpected happened. This way, the traders could continue to operate. The time of the month during which the POC was scheduled was also important. During this time, many unique technology events were occurring, such as increased network traffic due to options expiring and different applications being used.

Jason was glad he had deployed the POC. He could now take these next 10 days and clean up some outstanding issues that had been building in the digital certificate project. This would mean that he would spend less time using the biometric system, but the other project manager would be using it anyway.

The Methodology

When the POC group has been chartered, the goals and success criteria defined, and the vendors selected, it is time for the POC to be deployed. To maximize the value of the POC, the project team should treat the POC like it will be deployed enterprise-wide. This will give the team members a chance to explore issues like the following:

- Who does one call when something happens?–Using the biometric system like it would be used after deployment can expose these types of situations. Since we are in a POC phase, there is dedicated support to deal with the problems. At the same time, this provides valuable information to consider when planning the next phases of the project.
- What happens on the third day of every other month when the users stand on one foot and touch their noses?–In every organization, there are "special" situations that happen only so often. These special situations are normally the exception to every rule. Thus, the biometric system may need to be modified to meet this need. It is better to find out about these situations with only a handful of deployed users than to bring an entire company to a standstill because of an oversight.
- Will this be used on a daily basis?–By making desktop visits and analyzing the audit logs, team members can observe whether the users are prepared to accept the biometric system. It is better to find this out now, with little invested in the technology, than have millions sunk into a solution.
- Does this interfere with any mission-critical systems or applications?–Again, by setting the goals and success criteria early on, the critical applications that need support should have been included as part of the POC. Working seamlessly with critical applications should have been one of the success criteria for the project moving forward.
- Start talking to the desktop group about automated installations–Is there any funky stuff on the desktops to know about? Though the POC is deployed only to a handful of users, it is important to think of it as an enterprise solution. Therefore, now is the time to start thinking about corporate deployment. There is no use in having a workable solution if it cannot be deployed, or if existing software will interfere with the biometric system's installation.
- Talk to the server engineers about issues in deploying the authentication backend–If the biometric system needs to use a server for authentication or storage, it is important now to find out if the solution can be deployed on servers already running within the enterprise. The POC may have been installed by hand, with the help of a knowledgeable server engineer. If the project moves forward, future installs may need to be automated and "obvious" system adjustments made by the POC server engineer may need to be documented.

- Find out about architecture, the network, filesystems, and con-nectivity–During the POC phase, many different groups that may not normally interact are brought together as stakeholders. Now is the time to take advantage of this and brainstorm and discuss things such as architecture, network traffic, filesystems, and general connectivity issues.
- Talk to the risk management and IT security groups about their issues and concerns–Such discussions can help the project make adjustments for future stages, or allow the risk management and IT security groups to modify or create new risk and security pol-icies that will support the project going forward.

Following the above suggestions will ensure a high probability of the project's success from the project management perspective. This gives the technology a chance to prove itself without having interfer-ence from project management.

Monitor and Evaluate the POC

> Martin was glad he had assigned some of his staff to different stakeholders. The feedback was often gathered daily, sometimes hourly, on how the tech-nologies were performing. These extra resources gave Martin additional breathing room to spend time with some of the stakeholders himself, and personally follow up on emails of concern sent to him. He also had his staff collect and summarize the audit logs at the end of the POC.
>
> Jason was a whirlwind of activity. He tried to keep up with his digital signa-ture project and keep his fellow project managers working with the biomet-ric system. Jason's problems stemmed from the lack of time he and his colleagues really had to use the system. Most of the day was spent in meet-ings or on the phone. When they were at their desks, time was precious, and the unfamiliar biometric system was slowing them down; some were disabling the system, or avoiding it altogether.

The Methodology

Once the POC is deployed, it needs to be tended. This monitoring should include the following:

- Spend "quality time" with each group–It is important to make all stakeholders feel that they are being listened to and heard. This means having both formal and informal meetings and communications. Also, when out and about, listen for the hallway talk on how things are going. This can provide additional feedback that is not being passed through the POC group.

- Make sure needs are being heard and met–Spend time talking to the actual users of the biometric system. Calling and emailing is good for gathering general impressions on how things are going. Desk visits with face-to-face communication can give context to comments made on the phone or through email. Ask the user how he/she likes the system. Watch how the user uses the biometric system or, more importantly, see if the system has been deactivated or ignored.

- Be available as much as possible to troubleshoot and answer questions–Small problems and misconceptions can grow quickly. It is always easier to deal with a small grass fire than a raging inferno! There is only one opportunity to make a good first impression. Once that opportunity has been lost and a bad taste has been left in the mouth of the user, it is twice as hard to win the user back.

- Use the audit logs to gather additional empirical evidence of how the POC is going–Use the information presented in Chapter 4 to help understand the patterns being seen.

Monitoring and evaluating the POC can give first-hand data for making critical decisions.

Wrap Up the POC

Martin was pleased with how the POC was going. He prepared to send out his questionnaire. The questions were somewhat general in nature, but others were more pointed, based on his conversations with the stakeholders. The selection of the vendor was up to the POC participants and their responses to the questionnaire. As Martin had surmised, none of the vendors scored fully in every category, but all were in general pretty even. The difference to him and to his participants came down to problem response time. One company stood out from the others. This company was not the largest, but it was the most committed.

Jason was relieved the POC was finishing up. He needed to wrap it up quickly so he could get back to other issues, so he took the informal feedback from his colleagues and examined it. The feedback seemed for the most part undecided. None of the participants particularly hated the technology. With Jason's limited timeframes and resources, this was the best he could get.

The Methodology

The POC process is formal and structured, and the wrap of the POC needs to be treated the same way. To this end, the following suggestions may help:

- Inform the users on how to proceed until the next phase is decided–Since the biometric system is an integral part of the daily work of the end-users, they need to know what will happen to their use of the biometric system. Many users will want to continue using the biometric system. If this is not feasible, they need to be told why; if it is, an internal support structure needs to be put in place to support them. If the biometric system is to be decommissioned, then a plan needs to be communicated to the users and other concerned stakeholders about how this will occur.

- Wrap up the pilot with a questionnaire–The end-users of the project have spent the past 30–45 days with the biometric system. They want a chance to provide feedback and continue to be part of the process. Having suffered through some potential issues and problems, they want to be heard. The questionnaire needs to provide subjective and objective opportunities for feedback. The questions should be structured so that they will provide additional data to be used to determine if the performance criteria were met.

- Thank the users–The users need to be identified as an integral part of the process and to be recognized at the end through an email or a personal visit. If the project moves to the next phases, users will still be required to further validate the project. As such, the user population will need to grow. It is easier to expand the user population if the users from earlier phases feel that the experience was positive and their feedback was appreciated.

- Ask the users what they liked and didn't like–It is always easy to ask what people liked. It is more difficult to request and receive negative feedback. The project can succeed and move forward only if the shortcomings are recognized and then addressed. The shortcomings cannot be addressed if they are not solicited.

- The next step–The goal of the POC is to prove the technology and advance the process to the next phase. Asking the users how to accomplish the latter provides an opportunity for the project to receive feedback or may elicit new success criteria to be addressed in the next phase.

• Generate documentation–The information gathered from the POC needs to be recorded. This information should include the charter, the success criteria and goals, what the user environment was for testing, and lastly, the end-user feedback from the survey and other correspondence. Finally, and most importantly, it must include the recommendation of the POC group regarding the success criteria and goals from the charter. This document, in conjunction with the other documents, will provide the basis for evaluating each vendor's solution and finally making a go/no go decision.

With the POC formally completed and documented, an informed decision can be made on the next steps.

Decide on the Validity of Each Vendor's Solution

Martin looked at his survey results. Over 85% of his participants liked the technology and felt that it should proceed into a pilot. On top of that, there was an overwhelming 95% response rate to the survey. This indicated to Martin that this technology was fitting a very pressing need. Martin used the survey, his own experience, and the behavior of the vendors to make his selection.

Jason knew he had to get moving; the clock was ticking. He decided that the vendor was one he could work with and the solution did work pretty well for digital certificates. He assumed that it should work as well for other Windows-based passwords, and he hoped he was right, as he had very little time to try those features out.

The Methodology

Based on the documentation from the POC wrap-up, each vendor's product can be evaluated in light of the goals and success criteria. However, the vendor that met the most success criteria is not always the one selected. Often during the POC, one success criterion stands out as more important than the others. This could become a key in selecting the final product. Also, other intangibles like support and teamwork need to be considered in the decision. Once the decisions are made for each vendor, the next step can be taken.

Make a Go/No Go Decision to Move Ahead

Martin made his selection. He picked the vendor with the best survey results and the one he felt was most responsive to issues and problems. It is one thing to be quick to answer calls when things are going well; it is another when there are pressing technology issues. Martin informed his management and the participants of the decision, and tried to capture as much good will and momentum as possible.

Jason let his manager know the POC had been completed. It was generally felt by Jason's colleagues that the technology was a good idea. It was convenient and did replace the digital certificate password. When Jason was asked about the Windows password replacement, he said that it had worked well whenever they had a chance to use it.

The Methodology

Make a quick decision! There can only be two outcomes: Either the project moves forward or it is stopped. If the decision is a no go, then:

- Take time to look at alternate solutions—There is still a business need for this type of solution. As such, other solutions need to be sourced and vetted so that they may be considered for deployment.
- Give the vendor a clear message to move on—The vendor needs to be shown enough respect to be told that its solution is not moving forward. It needs to stop its investment in this opportunity and move on to the next one.
- Let the users know that they have been listened to—Most importantly, let the users know that they can make a difference. There is nothing worse than having a resounding round of "No's!" being ignored and moving ahead with a technology that is not wanted. By following this advice, you can go back to the users again to be part of the next POC.

If the decision is a go, then:

- Allow time to prepare for the next phase—A quick decision allows planning to begin sooner for the next phase of the project. The amount of time that can be condensed between phases reduces overall project time.
- Give the project time to engage additional resources, if needed— As the project moves into the next phase, the scale needs to

increase and more resources must be acquired to help mange, deploy, and support the next phases moving ahead.

- Let the users know that they have been listened to–There are times when the users want a particular technology and the company does not provide it. By letting the POC users know that the project is moving forward, they will know that their time and effort have not been wasted.

- Build on the existing momentum!–Most importantly, when a POC phase finishes positively, there is momentum in the company. There is talk and buzz about how well things went, and everyone wants to be associated with a winner. Thus, by moving quickly, the project can leverage this positive momentum and get the next phase moving quickly.

Announce the Results and Lay the Groundwork for the Next Phase

Martin was pleased to hear that senior management regarded the project as a great success. It felt that the pilot should be extended to more users across more trading groups. The reason for this was the buzz the project was generating. When one group of traders found out that others did not have to remember passwords anymore, they wanted in on the technology as well. So to meet the demand, the pilot would be expanded.

Jason was surprised at the response the biometric project got from senior management, which was in general pleased with the outcome. They felt that being a global company, a global perspective was needed in the pilot. It was recommended that the pilot be global in nature. Senior Management also wanted to involve groups from outside the project management team.

The Methodology

Regardless of the outcome of the POC phase, the results need to be made public. By doing this, the project is transparent in its operations and is seen as being positive to the overall morale of the company. With the announcement, the groundwork can be laid for either moving on to the next phase with the current technology or preparing for another POC.

Conclusion

The POC is an important part of getting a new technology deployed. The POC can be seen as the foundation on which everything else is built. In preparing for the POC, the project team needs to be as inclusive of all interested parties as possible. Clear goals and success criteria need to be defined, and the POC needs to be implemented like it is going to be deployed. The users of the POC need to be supported and have one-on-one time with the project group. Once it is time to wrap up the POC, information must be gathered from the POC users and other data sources should also be consulted. The results must be evaluated so that a vendor can be chosen. In choosing a vendor, a decision has been made to move the project forward. The user community and the company in general must be informed of the decision so that all positive momentum can be captured and built on.

13

Preparing for the Pilot Deployment

With the successful completion of the POC, the project now moves into the pilot phase. During this phase, the foundation laid by the POC is expanded as the basis for the pilot. The pilot tests the biometric system in terms of scale and deployability. Depending on the size of the company, the pilot may need to be multi-phased. In a multi-phased pilot, the follow-on pilots involve more users and additional applications for integration.

In preparing for the pilot phase, the following steps need to occur:

1. Define the group of stakeholders
2. Put in place a project management team that can see the solution through to rollout
3. Form and charter the pilot group
4. Develop policy documents
5. Summarize daily reports weekly and send them out
6. Address and track problems and solutions as they occur
7. Put a training plan in place
8. Prepare audit and analysis reports
9. Build and test an automated install
10. Roll out the software and hardware in a practical manner
11. Provide mechanisms for feedback
12. After initial pilot rollout, get the executives involved
13. Address issues of scalability and manageability for rollout
14. Near the end of the pilot, discuss the next steps
15. Wrap up the pilot

16. Make a go/no go decision

17. Build a transition book

As in the previous chapter, the examples of Martin and Jason will be used.

Define the Group of Stakeholders

> Martin was ready to include a larger cross-section of the trader community. Martin spoke with his team and paired off the new stakeholders with stakeholders from the POC phase. This way, Martin could spread the load of bringing new people up to speed on the nature of the pilot and what the technology could and could not do.
>
> Jason examined the proposed list of participants put forward by senior management. The names on the list encompassed four continents and virtually every line of business the company had. Jason had no internal colleagues he could use to help him get the others up to speed. The best Jason could do was hire some consultants from the selected vendor to assist him. Since the budget was disappearing quickly, the number of days that he would like to have for the vendors was reduced by half. This meant that Jason would need to get some volunteer regional help to manage and support the local pilot community.

The Methodology

The stakeholders for the pilot will include the same ones from the POC, but will be expanded to include any new business units that are part of the pilot. The roles are the same as before, but the scope and the impact of the decisions made are larger. The decisions made here will impact how the biometric system will be rolled out for the enterprise.

Put in Place a Project Management Team That Can See the Solution Through to Rollout

> Martin knew from the start who would comprise the project team. He had planned for himself and his direct reports to see this through until the end. The "head time" this project was receiving from senior executives was increasing. They were seeing this as a possible company-wide solution if all went well.

As Jason and his handful of consultants flew to Scotland for the first pilot implementation, he had a knot in his stomach. How could he possibly get this pilot deployed in the time he had been given? He needed to get to 4 different continents and 7 different cities in less than 15 days. This did not give him a lot of time to do anything. He also knew that if this pilot was successful, he would need to hand it off to a production team. He had no one from production even listed as part of the pilot.

The Methodology

The pilot group will learn a lot about deploying the biometric system, and it would be ideal to leverage that experience for the deployment. The group chosen by the stakeholders to be the project management team should be able to see the project through from the pilot to the deployment stage. By doing this, the speed and confidence with which the deployment will occur are increased.

Form and Charter the Pilot Group

Martin examined what was asked of his group for the pilot. The senior executives wanted more trading groups involved. Martin adjusted the roles of everyone involved. He assigned himself to be the liaison with a new trading group that was joining the pilot. This left his senior manager to handle the day-to-day management follow-up that he had done for the POC. The supported applications would not change for the pilot. Choosing additional applications to support would be done on a case-by-case basis, and only ones that clearly had no support impact would be added. The biggest hurdle was to keep expectations in line. With the success of the POC, there were very high expectations for the pilot. These expectations would need to be managed.

Jason planned to not expand the roles and responsibilities of the pilot group if it could be avoided. With the limited time in each continent and city, looking at anything new was out of the question. Jason wanted the users to have low expectations for the pilot. This way, if his group could under-promise and over-deliver, the project may make it through okay.

The Methodology

The pilot charter will include all the elements of the POC charter, with the following additions or changes:

- Expanded roles and responsibilities–Since the scope of the pilot is much larger, the roles and responsibilities are greater as well. To accommodate this, individual stakeholders will consult more with their direct reporting lines. That is, the members of the stakeholder group will consult more frequently with their senior managers and executives. In addition, the internal sponsor of the project and the senior executive sponsor will take more active roles in the project. Since the stakes are now higher, so are the risks and rewards. With the success of the POC, all concerned want to see success once again.
- Define new goals and success criteria for this phase–The goals and success criteria will be very similar to the POC, but the scope will be much greater. The goals will generalize somewhat to support the greater scope, and the success criteria will be more objective than subjective. It is much easier to evaluate numerous objective answers than numerous subjective answers.
- Manage users and support expectations–With the success of the pilot, the unofficial bar for success will be set higher internally. It is now more important than ever to manage expectations. If expectations are set too high, then the smallest sign of failure could impede the entire project. On the other hand, setting expectations too low will result in the usefulness of the pilot being called into question. Executives and users involved in the project may think that the pilot is just a remake of the POC. There may also be an expectation set with the users that support for the pilot will occur through normal mechanisms.
- Get buy-in from all concerned groups–While this seems like a standard thing to get from all stakeholders, it becomes easier to ignore people or groups that dissent with the majority view. If one group is dissenting based on its point of view, that group is easier to ignore, as there is a large enough user base to get agreement without including the troublesome group. The danger of doing this is isolating that particular group and losing its support and input.

Develop Policy Documents

> Martin was now making daily notes and updates to a list of policy documents that needed to be maintained. In expanding the pilot, the team had discovered a number of anomalies and issues. It was important to start outlining these in point form so that Martin or someone on his team could take over the document and create it.
>
> Jason sucked in his breath slowly. The first machine they had installed failed on a reboot. It seemed that the Windows domain configuration in Europe was different from that in North America. This uncovered a corporate policy that should have been documented and distributed to all European sites, but there was no time to do such a thing now.

The Methodology

Now that the group of users involved in the pilot is much larger than the POC group, official policy documents need to be created based on the feedback and experiences of the POC group. Some of the policy documents include:

- Dealing with a mixed environment—With the increase in scope for the pilot, there will be a larger number of users involved. With this larger installed base, there are now issues of piloting in a mixed environment. This means that documents need to be created to explain how to work in a mixed environment.
- Support responsibilities—The support infrastructure needs to be able to handle a larger installed user base. It is no longer feasible to have the IT support stakeholders themselves providing support. A support group needs to be created using the normal support structure of the company. Members of the IT support group should already be familiar with the biometric system from their POC involvement. By involving them in the POC and making them stakeholders, a successful support groundwork has been laid.
- Pilot selection criteria—Since the POC group was smaller, it was easier to decide who should be a part of the POC. With the larger scale of the pilot, it will no longer be feasible to know each participant. Thus, pilot user selection criteria need to be created which should include technological requirements, business function requirements, user's availability for the pilot timeframe requirements, and lastly, the willingness to accept

possibly unstable software on the user's desktop. Most users want to have the latest and greatest software, so there will be no end of volunteers for the project. The project team needs to set a maximum number of users. This number of users is chosen so that there is a large enough sampling of users to be representative of the user population, yet small enough that the new IT support infrastructure can scale up to meet the support demand.

- Brochures and documents for pilot users—While it is very unlikely that any end-user ever reads documentation, a good tri-fold brochure is likely to be referenced occasionally. This brochure should list the support numbers to call, the manager of the project, the goals of the project, how the user interacts with the new hardware and software, and how long the pilot is going to last. More detailed documentation can be created and given to the users when they have completed their training. These documents should be in reference format and should cover the most frequently asked questions and the most common tasks.

- Guidelines for dealing with remote and laptop users—With the need to provide flexible work arrangements and the need for employees to travel, policy documents must cover remote and laptop users. The pilot must be representative of the entire user population. Thus, at some point during the pilot, the remote and laptop users' needs should be addressed. Perhaps the project team will decide that remote and laptop users are outside the scope of the project. If that is the case, the policy documents should state this.

- Security policies—With the implementation of any new security offering, current policies and procedures may need updating, or new ones may need to be created. These changes could be caused by the new methodologies being used or features that the biometric system offers. For example, one security policy may state that after three authentication attempts, the user account must be locked. With a biometric system, this may not be feasible. A user may take more than three attempts to verify while becoming habituated, or the biometric itself may have a high failure-to-verify rate. In addition, an old policy may have been put into place to prevent brute-force attacks on passwords. Biometrics, on the other hand, are not susceptible to brute-force attacks like passwords. Thus, such a policy will need to be updated.

Summarize Daily Reports Weekly and Send Them Out

With the current size of the pilot, it was no longer feasible for Martin to keep everyone personally informed. At the same time, Martin's need to have the latest information was even more pressing. He asked everyone to send him daily reports. These reports contained information on current deployments, plus any issues and resolutions. If someone had seen the daily reports, he/she would have thought the wheels had come off. With the complete picture of what was going on, Martin knew that what he was reading daily was the right information. The information was too detailed to send to senior executives. Martin instead summarized and sent out the data to the senior executives weekly. Martin then joined their conference call the following week to provide additional feedback and answer any outstanding questions.

Jason needed to keep his manager informed. With the limited time he had, he emailed quick updates to his manager. With little context available around some of his emails, there was generally a gloomy feel to the whole project. His updates always seemed to indicate they were falling behind and leaving some machines half installed because of unresolved issues.

The Methodology

With the larger scale of the project and the greater number of people involved, it is not practical to share knowledge and information in an *ad hoc* way. With the larger scale, there are always new problems to overcome and lessons to be learned everyday. This type of information needs to be collected, consolidated, and reported. There can be tactical daily reports that track day-to-day activities and issues. These reports should get summarized at the end of each week. The summarized report should be sent to all the stakeholders, the project management group, and to the senior executive group. This way, the executives can read the report if they choose and will feel included during the pilot. This feeling of inclusion is important as the larger final decision of moving ahead with deployment is made. If the senior executives have felt included, it will be easier for them to support whatever recommendation the stakeholders come back with.

Address and Track Problems and Solutions As They Happen

Martin had started his own tracking system. Every issue that came in on the daily reports was listed and tracked. With the increasing size of the project, and the complexity of some of the bugs, Martin could not accurately track them manually. To resolve this issue, he worked with the vendor to get access to its bug system so he could examine in real time, at his pace, the current status of the open bugs.

Jumping time zones was tough enough, but not even staying in place long enough to be contacted was worse. With the lightning-like pace Jason needed to keep up, it was not surprising that it was taking him upwards of 24 hours to respond to an issue. To address this issue, Jason created an internal discussion group. It was his hope that the pilot community could post and share issues and resolutions. Problem tracking was done in the evenings on the rare nights when the group returned early enough.

The Methodology

Beyond the reporting and tracking described, additional attention needs to be paid to problem and resolution tracking. As the pilot is deployed, issues will arise that must be addressed. It is important to record when a problem was first seen, on what desktop build, on what biometric system configuration, the severity of the problem, and lastly, the resolution. This type of information should be shared as quickly as possible and will form the basis of a support database. The better the data in the support database, the more efficient the support infrastructure. Thus, when a problem is seen again by a different support resource, he/she can consult the support database and see the resolution to the problem. Beyond providing a support reference, tracking the problems shows that both issues and resolutions are being found. Documenting this will allow claims of outstanding issues to be refuted at the end of the pilot. The issue log also shows that the pilot is doing what it was intended to do, that is, to find, document, and correct the issues of the biometric system before full-scale deployment.

Put a Training Plan in Place

> Martin realized that training was important to the success of the pilot. He also knew that his team did not have the expertise or the time to create customized training. Martin contracted the vendor to reproduce and deliver a number of training courses tailored to his pilot community. This way, the users received first-class training, and his staff was free to keep the warm and fuzzies going.
>
> Jason had planned ahead for training. He had the vendor create a personal training course that could be given to each user and administrator. Unfortunately, the consultants wanted four hours of training, but had to settle for two. Jason hoped this bootstrap training would carry the clients through to deployment, when a corporate training plan could be put in place.

The Methodology

Training is quite often the first thing to slide when new technology is put in place. It is also one of the most important aspects for a pilot and future deployments to be successful. Trained users have confidence in the product. Training also provides a controlled environment for user habituation. For the training to be successful for both the end-user and company, the following should be considered:

- Train the initial pilot users—While this seems obvious, it is quite often not done. By training the initial pilot users, the training itself is also piloted. What seemed like an important area to cover may turn out not to be. What seemed insignificant may generate lots of questions. This type of feedback occurs only when the course is delivered. Getting this feedback early on will make the deployment training better. If bad training is provided for a product, that information spreads quickly within the user community. Once this happens, it will be difficult to get users to attend. If, on the other hand, the training is seen to be useful and focused, it will be easier to attract attendees.
- Train the help desk in support issues—Again, this step needs to occur. There are already some members of the help desk who were part of the initial POC. They are a good group to ask what type of training should be done, and in what areas of the biometric system should support training be focused. Maybe they found from the POC that knowing how to properly enroll the biometric and subsequently how to verify were very important.

Information like this can be used to build the customized training for the help desk. Providing the help desk with training also helps overcome initial fears and concerns.

- Customize and focus the training on the features being used–
  Quite often, when a biometric system is being considered for use, the entire function and feature set of the system are not used. There is no use in training on features and functionality that will not be used.

- Realize that time is a limited commodity with the above groups–The training message needs to be concise and presented clearly. Customizing the training for both end-users and support personnel will limit the time needed to deliver the knowledge both groups need to be successful.

- Have a focused message and stick to it–It is very easy to get sidetracked while presenting training. This is especially true if the technology is cutting-edge. It is easy to get off on tangential discussions about company direction with the technology and future biometric system direction. What is important is to keep focused on the overall message of the training. At the same time, it may be worthwhile having more detailed conversations around an important question or concern. Remember, the training is meant to indoctrinate and habituate the users to the system. When the users feel comfortable with the training, this will be easier to accomplish.

- Provide additional take-away materials–While it will not be possible to cover every aspect of the system to be used, it is important to at least document that information in a concise and usable way. In addition, giving the user something to take away when he/she leaves can increase confidence in the system. This way, the user has something to consult when he/she has problems. Many times, the user has a very simple question and does not want to bother the help desk with it or is too embarrassed to ask. Having this documentation will help.

- Follow up with students 4–7 days later for additional questions–
  While the training course was presented in a clear and concise manner, time may have been limited and the pace of the training may have been rather quick. This does not lend itself well to the end-user's being able to take it all in and come up with questions on the spot. Follow up with students with a personal visit, if possible, to allow for questions to be asked. It can also offer an

opportunity to solicit direct feedback on the course, or to allow the user to ask any additional questions.

Training is an integral part of the success of the pilot and the future deployment. After training, the users feel informed and empowered. In addition, the training itself gets a chance to be piloted, and if necessary, adjusted before being given in support of the deployment.

Prepare Audit and Analysis Reports

> Martin once again looked at the daily updates he was receiving. Every install and every problem that was resolved or outstanding was documented. With these reports, he could provide anyone with an up-to-the-day snapshot of where the project stood.
>
> Jason looked at his email inbox and sighed. Every message was about the pilot, and none looked too happy. He tried to get update emails out, but had little time to do so.

The Methodology

Since this biometric system is probably new to the company, there will be no existing audit and analysis reports for it. The biometric system itself may have some audit and analysis functionality, which needs to be examined and understood. By doing this, it can be determined what type of information can be collected and analyzed. Once this information is available, existing audit and analysis reports can be leveraged. For example, if there is an audit report created every month that shows user creation and deletion, it is more than likely that the risk management and/or audit group will want similar reports. Additionally, creating these reports now will demonstrate that the project is moving ahead toward rollout. An enterprise system cannot be deployed if it cannot be audited and analyzed. The reports generated during the pilot for audit and analysis will also be useful in making final decisions on success criteria and goal attainment.

Build and Test an Automated Install

Martin had included the client engineering team from the start, so a number of people from the group had been examining the biometric system software. This way, when it came time for an automated install, some thought had already been put into it.

Jason was starting to understand why each geographic region repackaged software from other regions. There were no common standards followed among these European sites, from the service packs on their machines to the domain infrastructure being used. When an automated install was built for one area, no one told the installers that the software needed to be installed as the default GINA module. Thus, the vendor software could not be activated. For the POC, it was practical to do software installation and configuration by hand, but it was no longer feasible for the pilot or deployment. The sheer number of desktops to be deployed prevented manual installs from being practical. Thus, an automated install method and distribution method had to be tested and used. Every major corporation already had in place a software distribution and installation system. The software portion of the biometric system needed to leverage this existing infrastructure. Thus, the software had to be packaged using installer software and prepared for distribution using the company's distribution system. This entailed many iterations of testing and refinement to get right. The pilot provided an opportunity to test what was believed to be the final version before deployment.

The Methodology

It is better to have the install fail on a couple of hundred desktops than on thousands or tens of thousands of desktops. In addition, by using the automated procedure during the pilot, any possible desktop configuration and already installed software issues can be identified and addressed. It goes without saying that an uninstall also needs to be possible. In the future, the software may need to be upgraded or removed if the pilot does not move ahead to deployment. If possible, a "cleaner" utility also needs to be created, which allows for the low-level removal of a product, even if it is not fully installed. It can stop running tasks and services and uninstall the software in a direct way from both the registry and the directory. Thus, this utility could be used when an install aborts in some way and the uninstall program will not run.

Roll Out the Software and Hardware in a Practical Manner

The order in which Martin would roll out the hardware and software was quite straightforward. As each trading unit was distinct, it was easy to schedule and deliver the installation of both the hardware and software. Hardware could be installed at any time in the future and activated after the software was installed.

Jason had a challenge in front of him. Since the biometric project was tied to the digital certificate project, the order of rollout was *ad hoc*. Any employee could apply for and receive a digital certificate on-the-fly. That meant that the hardware needed to be put out as early as possible.

The Methodology

Once the automated install is ready and the pilot user selection is complete, it is time to get the pilot deployed. The deployment order of the pilot needs to be done according to the enterprise's needs. This ordering of the pilot rollout may be done in the following ways:

- By business line–The pilot community should cover as many types of users as possible to give an overall representative sample. The order of deployment does not have to cover all parts of the user community at once. It may make sense to deploy along business unit lines. that is, a certain business unit may be easier to do first. It may also be required that the entire pilot population of that business unit be completed at the same time. This could be for reasons of compatibility with each others' business processes, to support a free or hot seating model, or because it is simply a good time for the unit to be deployed.
- By level of effort required for installation–It may be known from the POC that one particular desktop build or business unit will be easier to get working than another. In this way, the pilot would be rolled out from the easiest to the hardest. This allows the pilot to build momentum, confidence, and success. Then, when the pilot deployment hits difficulty with more challenging deployments, there will be confidence in the solution, and troubleshooting and resolution will be easier.
- By risk of failure–Like level of effort, the risk of failure of the biometric system or the desktops of the pilot users must be evaluated. Users for whom the risk of failure is high within the context of the business or who would have a high downtime cost

should be deployed last. By that point, most issues with the pilot deployment should have been identified and addressed, and additional support resources will be available to help support these high-risk users. Also, it goes without saying that the executive users should not be done too early. Senior executives quite often want the latest software and hardware before anyone else. In doing this too soon, the additional resources required to support the executives would impact the ability to deliver support to the rest of the pilot community. Like other riskier users, they should be done near the end of the pilot.

The final decision on how the pilot will be deployed may be influenced by all, some, or none of the above. Also, it is important to be flexible and change how the pilot is deployed as it moves forward. It is of no use making mistakes if you cannot learn from them and adjust. Thus, the deployment plan is only a plan; as such, it may need to be changed and updated as it moves forward.

Provide Mechanisms for Feedback

With the expanded project team Martin put in place, it was easy for a pilot user to give feedback to a team member. This feedback was then summarized and sent to Martin. When Martin got the feedback, he could make on-the-fly changes to how something was done or arrange for a desk visit to address the issue.

Jason could not keep up with the email coming in. The use of a discussion news group seemed like a good idea at the time. Unfortunately, it was full of more questions than answers. The group had been made open, and thus anyone could read or post. It was unfortunate, but some were getting a bad impression of the technology without ever using it. Jason knew that for this method to work, he needed a knowledgeable discussion moderator.

The Methodology

The users need to be able to voice their issues and concerns in as many ways as possible. Some issues are best expressed in open, anonymous forums, and others face-to-face. What follows are some suggestions on starting and keeping the lines of communication open among the pilot user community and the project and support groups:

- Email group–Most corporate email systems support groups. Creating groups to send questions to, or to distribute information to, is easy and convenient. By using a group email address, all participants or concerned parties will get the email. That is to say, an end-user may not know all the project members, but if the user is told to use ProjTeam as the email group, it will reach all the right people. The same holds true for the project and support teams. Using email groups makes sure everyone is kept informed who needs to be.

- Discussion folder—The use of a discussion forum allows a hierarchical view of the conversations and questions, It can also offer the users and others the chance to share information or concerns anonymously. This way, all issues and questions can be shared for everyone to learn from. It can also provide a source of information to update the frequently-asked-questions-list, and supply additional data for the support database.

- Phone number for support and questions—Nothing ever replaces hearing another human voice in real time. The ability to reach live support people on the first call cannot be stressed enough. Pilots and piloting software can be very stressful on the end-user, especially when things go wrong. Thus, picking up the phone and talking to someone to get support can help reduce the stress and tension of the situation. These phone numbers and the fact that a live support person will answer will also increase the user's confidence in using the system, decreasing his/her fear of using the system and having something happen and being stuck.

- Random desk visits to solicit feedback directly—While providing as many means of communication as possible is very good, nothing beats a desktop visit. By visiting the user in his/her environment, you get to see first-hand how the system is used, and also the user may be stimulated to say or ask something he/she may not have communicated otherwise. It also makes the user feel appreciated, which is an important part of the process.

Stress the importance of hearing from the users what they like, but most importantly, also elicit feedback on what they don't like! This should be stressed at every opportunity to communicate with the users. Nothing will slow or possibly derail a pilot faster than simmering rumors of problems or general dissatisfaction. The only way to get this resolved is to encourage users to voice their concerns on anything and everything. Share the water-cooler gossip about the project so that rumors can be quieted and real issues identified and resolved. By doing this, it creates a healthy working environment and puts a stop to possible dissention in the user community.

When a problem is resolved, there should be a follow-up with users to make sure the solution was acceptable and really did solve the problem. This is probably the most important step in problem resolution after finding a solution. Many times, solutions need to come from people who have no direct end-user interaction or experience. As such, the solutions sometimes solve the problem from a purely technical standpoint, but are not acceptable to the end-users. For example, a problem may be identified where the biometric system hangs. The solution may be to either reboot the machine or disable the software causing the conflict. While both solutions resolve the problem, one may be more acceptable to the user than the other. The software that needs to be disabled may be crucial to the user's duties. The failure may be seen only intermittently, so rebooting is not a big deal. The converse of this is that the end-user may need to consider accepting the solution if that is the only one available. The user may also be given the opportunity to be removed from the pilot. Offering this option can at many times make the problem less significant. For example, if the biometric system has made the user's daily activities much easier and less stressful, having to deal with a small glitch may be preferable to losing the benefit of the system entirely.

The importance of getting user feedback cannot be overstated; just as important is using the user feedback. The users need to see actions and problem resolutions coming out of their feedback. If they do not, they will most likely stop the flow of communication.

After Initial Pilot Rollout, Get the Executives Involved

Martin was ready to take his project to the executives. To prepare for this, the support team for the senior executives was part of the project for weeks ahead of time. This way, if there was anything funny on the desktops they supported, they might be able to catch it. It was unlikely that Martin and his team would be allowed to do the install, so Martin arranged for one of his senior technical people to be with the senior executive support staff during the install.

Jason could not even contemplate getting an executive installed. He did not have the bandwidth or the time. The Windows password replacement was acting up, and many were having a tough time enrolling.

The Methodology

As discussed in deciding on the order of pilot rollout, executives were to be left to the end of the pilot because of the associated support requirements. Now that the pilot deployment is nearing completion, and the initial speed bumps have been overcome, the executives can be brought online. At this point, the pilot has had some wins and momentum has built. The executives have undoubtedly heard this and are eager to get installed. Their enthusiasm for the project can be used to help mitigate any problems that may arise. If they are excited about the technology, small inconveniences that may have seemed larger earlier on will barely get mentioned. Because they were deployed near the end, the executives will have fresh, positive experiences in mind when it comes time to sign off on deployment.

Start Addressing Issues of Scalability and Manageability for Rollout

Martin had always treated the POC and pilot like they were deployments. In this way, issues of manageability and scalability could be discussed with the vendor while the pilot went on. And, when it came time to do a deployment, all these issues had already been addressed.

Jason looked at the calendar and realized that it was Wednesday afternoon on the second to last day of the trip. He had many outstanding issues to still address, the least of which was defining the resources needed for support and deployment. Deploying an executive was out of the question.

The Methodology

As the pilot comes online, the issues of scalability and manageability come to the forefront. During the POC, the user population was relatively small and easy to manage in a distributed way. Also, the infrastructure needs were minimal. Now that there may be many more users, scalability and manageability will be tested. To help in recognizing these needs, the following questions should be asked:

- Do we need additional infrastructure?—As the pilot starts consuming the current infrastructure, it will become clear whether the current infrastructure will support the pilot and possible future rollout. Is the authentication server or database server able to handle the authentication demands? Are the networks able to handle the extra bandwidth, especially at peak times of the day? Answers to these types of questions will allow the project team to decide if the infrastructure needs to be upgraded for a rollout to occur. By finding this out now, the infrastructure can be upgraded in a planned and controlled way.

- What changes do we need to make to the installation package?—It may become evident that certain tweaks are necessary to make it run smoother. Special installation cases may be identified, and original assumptions may be proved wrong. If possible, these changes should be made to the package during the pilot deployment and tested on the outstanding pilot desktops.

- Is the user initialization scaling?—For the end-users to start using the biometric system, they need to initialized. This initialization may range from user creation in a database to the addition of a schema to an existing LDAP directory. If the current methods for implementation seem cumbersome or time-consuming for the pilot, then they must be modified to scale for a potential rollout.

- Do we need additional support personnel?—As the pilot is deployed to many more users, a general level of user support will set in. There will be an initial surge in support requests at the start of the pilot. As this declines over time, there will be a general leveling off in calls. This new level needs to be sustained. This information can be extrapolated to the projected size of the deployment, and will in turn provide the number of support personnel required to move forward.

- Can this be centrally managed?—This is very important for general deployment. It will not be practical to visit every desktop or part of the company for general management of the biometric solution, so the biometric solution being tested needs to be centrally managed. If it is not currently feasible to do this, is the vendor willing to support centralized management? What mitigating steps can be taken internally until centralized support is provided?

The sooner in the pilot that issues of scalability and manageability can be addressed, the easier it will be to prepare for deployment. In addition, scalability and manageability are more than likely important success criteria that need to be met. By gathering this information early on, it can be used to help in the evaluation.

Near the End of the Pilot, Start Discussing the Next Steps

Martin could feel the momentum this pilot had Overall, it was a success. He began tentative discussions with the vendor on some additional features and bug fixes he would need to be able to recommend this product for deployment.

Jason looked at the handful of vendor consultants and laughed. He knew that even if he had three times the number of consultants that he had now, the pilot and POC would need to be redone.

The Methodology

Since the scale of the pilot is much larger than the POC, general consensus will build more rapidly about the project. In addition, since the pilot will last longer then the POC, objective data will build more quickly. This allows for trends to be charted and projections to be made about the outcome. This information can be used to start the discussions on attaining the goals and meeting the success criteria. These preliminary discussions will lay the groundwork for a final executive decision on the rollout. It will also be an indication of how probable a rollout will be. If it is looking positive, then preliminary planning can begin. If it looks like the rollout will not be approved, then a decommission plan can be prepared for presentation. Either way, do not wait for a decision to be made. Anticipate the decision and either build on the momentum currently underway or prepare to dismantle the project quickly and efficiently.

Wrap Up the Pilot

Martin wrapped up the pilot by hosting a bash at the local watering hole. He again sent out a survey to the user population to gauge the feedback.

Jason prepared to return to North America. It would be a long flight home, as the technology had not been up to the pilot. Jason gathered his notes and thoughts and mentally prepared for the next step.

The Methodology

The methodology used to conclude the pilot is exactly the same as for the POC.

Make a Go/No Go Decision

For Martin, the senior executive blessing was a mere formality. He had delivered on what was requested of him with glowing feedback from the pilot participants.

When Jason returned to North America from his trip, he could smell blood in the water and the sharks were circling. The biometric project was collapsing in on itself. There was nothing at this point he could do to prevent it. The issues were systemic and they ran deep. Now was not the time to take this technology to the world.

The Methodology

As with the POC, make a quick decision! There are still only two outcomes: Either the project moves forward or it stops.

If the decision is a no go, then:

- Give time to decommission–There will be a significant amount of infrastructure that needs dismantling, along with the user workstations, which need to be restored to the pre-pilot state. In addition, the biometric data collected must be securely disposed of or deleted.
- Give the vendor a clear message to move on–The vendor should be shown enough respect to be told that its solution is not moving forward, at which point it can stop its investment in this opportunity and move on to the next one.
- Let the users know that they have been heard–Most importantly, let the users know that they made a difference. There is nothing worse than having a resounding round of "No's!" being ignored and a technology that is not wanted moving ahead. By following this advice, you can go back to the users again to be part of the next POC.

If the decision is a go, then:

- Give time to prepare for the next phase–A quick decision allows planning to begin sooner for the next phase of the project. The amount of time that can be condensed between phases reduces the overall project time.
- Give the project time to get additional resources engaged, if needed–As the project moves into the next phase, the scale needs to increase. As the scale increases, more resources must

be acquired to help manage, deploy, and support the next phases moving ahead.

- Let the users know that they have been heard–There are times when the users want a particular technology and the company does not provide it. By letting the pilot users know that the project is moving forward, you let them know that their time and effort have not been wasted.
- Build on the existing momentum!–Most importantly, when a pilot finishes positively, there is momentum in the company. There is talk and buzz about how well things went, and everyone wants to be part of a winner. Thus, by moving quickly, the project can leverage this positive momentum and get the next phase moving quickly

Build a Transition Book

Martin looked at the stack of printouts and his own notebook and wondered if any more information could possibly come in before the transition could take place. He had collected and learned an amazing amount of information. The book could be enhanced by everyone on the team.

Jason knew the transition book he needed to prepare. It was the type of transition book that you would rarely want to make. This transition book was the closing of the pilot. The pilot needed to be safely decommissioned and the workstations reconfigured to their original settings.

The Methodology

Once a go decision has been made, the stakeholders need to step back and let the project progress. While it is ideal to keep the same project management team, the responsibility of deployment now rests with the production portion of the IT group. It is this group's mandate to get solutions deployed. They are the experts on deploying systems and need to make their own deployment decisions. The last deliverable by the stakeholders and project management team is a transition book. The transition book needs to include the following information:

- All known biometric system configurations–This needs to include any and all system parameters and server configurations. What access rights are required and where the software and hardware can be found also need to be documented.

- All desktop incompatibilities–During the pilot, certain desktop incompatibilities will be found. These need to be documented and workarounds identified. Since the deployment is being taken over by production, there may be changes in the environment that can be made to allow the deployment to be easier.
- Documentation of the automated installs–It is most likely that the pilot automated installs were built with input from the production group, so the group is probably quite familiar with them. It is still proper form to document them and to communicate where on the network they are located.
- A list of frequently asked questions–The frequently asked questions from the POC and pilot will aid the production group in the rollout. These are the questions that the group needs to be most aware of, and in turn, the group can leverage the collected experience of everyone.
- The knowledge repository–During the pilot, a support knowledge repository is built. This is invaluable technical information that the production group can use. It can again provide information about the environment and workarounds used.
- Training courses–A training course needs to be created for the production group and delivered at the group's request.
- Tips and tricks–During the POC and pilot, certain "trade" knowledge will be developed. This information includes the undocumented items that will make deployment easier. For example, this could include third-party tools for troubleshooting, changes that can be made to user systems to make them run better, or adjustments that can be made to make the deployment experience better.
- Recommendations for deployment and for the next project– The collected knowledge from the POC and pilot needs to be surveyed for recommendations for a successful rollout and to determine what changes should be made to the project framework for the next project.

Conclusion

Martin felt relief. For the first time in a long while, he could relax. Martin and his team had delivered on the goals and requirements of the project. The pilot was a huge success. As the pilot was deployed, more and more business units wanted to be part of it. At first, the team tried to accommodate as many as they could. In the end, many business units had to wait for deployment. With a good core of solid work done and a transition book ready, Martin could relax and know that the deployment would go smoothly.

Jason rubbed his weary, jet-lagged eyes and met with his manager. They had no choice but to stop the pilot. The failing could be traced back to the POC. The decisions made there would follow Jason and his team through the pilot. The change in the goals of the pilot by adding the need for other password replacement should have caused the POC to be extended. The fact that the digital certificates were a global project involving all lines of business should have spurred Jason to include groups outside of project management. Once the scope of the pilot was changed to global, the senior manager should have asked for more budget and resources. When Jason first started having problems in Europe, he should have slowed down and addressed them then and there. By moving on and not fixing the problems, he left one area in a bad state and started another with possibly the same outcome. The root cause of the failure was having to start a major project that was coupled with an existing project entering its deployment stage. This caused extra pressure and time constraints on the new project to play quick catch-up with the original project. This forced corners to be cut and steps to be skipped in the methodology.

The pilot is the transition point from the POC to the rollout. It builds on the foundation laid by the POC and validates the technology on a larger scale. This validation must take into account all aspects of the solution and its suitability for rollout. In this phase, more time is spent simulating a rollout and anticipating what questions will be asked and answered. Methodologies for deployment, user indoctrination, training, and support are refined and modified. Lastly, once the pilot is deployed and functioning, discussions begin on making a go/no go decision. Based on those discussions, a general indication is given on the next step. If it is a go, then additional work begins on gathering the information required for the transition to a rollout and the transition book is started. If the pilot is not moving forward, then plans are made to quickly and effectively decommission the existing pilot infrastructure.

Most importantly, however, the pilot is the last chance to get things right. By the time the project gets to the rollout stage, all the major problems should have been overcome and a deployment methodology should be known and tested.

14

Preparing
for the Rollout

Congratulations! Your project has made it this far. Now is the time to see the fruits of your labor. By this stage in the project, all the heavy lifting has been done, all the tough decisions have been made; now is the time to execute the rollout plan. The following suggestions will help the rollout proceed:

- Modify the project plan from the pilot to include lessons learned–The rollout plan needs to leverage all prior experiences. During the pilot, the deployment methodology may have worked for some portions of the pilot community, but not for others. You may have discovered that the hardware deployment takes longer than anticipated. These types of things need to be incorporated into the rollout plan.

- Acquire and deploy any additional resources–From the scalability results and the support results of the pilot, additional resources may have been projected for the rollout. If so, at the start of the rollout, or as the pilot is finishing, acquire and train these new resources. The project needs all its resources to hit the ground running.

- Build a rollout schedule that can be met–This cannot be stressed enough. With all the preparation, there should be a very good understanding of how long activities take. This should be reflected in the rollout schedule. Now that the project has hit the rollout phase, the finance group and the executives will be watching for delays and cost over-runs. With proper project planning and rollout scheduling, these risks can be minimized. In addition, it is best to ramp up the rollout. Since this could possibly be the first deployment for the production team, time must be allowed for the team to make some mistakes. By not having a heavy deployment schedule up-front, more time can be spent getting it right the first time and developing a healthy deployment methodology.

- Don't be afraid to push off the deployment date if there are uncompleted or untested steps—The rollout needs to be delayed until they are addressed. The rollout must leverage the work already done and the lessons learned from previous experiences. If something is encountered for the first time during the rollout, the timeframes for resolution are shorter. Thus, it cannot be stressed enough that no steps can be skipped in the pilot or POC stages.

- Have more than enough support staff available to respond after an area is deployed—When the go-live date occurs, there is normally an initial time period when user support requirements are high. These support requirements can range from installation and configuration issues to questions about the technology. The project support group needs to have more than enough staff available to meet the surge in demand. After the initial surge, support should level off again, as experienced in the pilot, though at a higher level.

- Document so this project can be handed off to support—When the project moved from pilot to rollout, a transition book was created. The same thing needs to be done for support. The existing transition book can form the basis of the one given to support. This support transition book should include items like the following:

  - How the software gets patched—Once the software is packaged in an automated install, bug fixes and enhancement patches will come along. How these get put into the production system depends on the requirements of the support group and how involved a patch is. If the patch involves simple file replacement, then the new file could be distributed through an automated means, or the existing automated package could be updated. If the patch is more involved than simple file replacement, a secondary automated install may be created. This secondary install should be run after the original automated install. Lastly, any changes to the rollout production systems need to be documented and tested. Since not all users may receive the patch file, there must be a way to identify the users who have the patch. This could be done through the use of a support database that lists the names of users or files to get version numbers from. Preferably, the biometric system has some method to obtain version numbers and patch levels. Even if this information is stored in the registry, automated means could be created to retrieve this information for use by the support group.

- Who to contact if the IT support group needs support—While IT personnel are seen in general as the support authorities, they cannot possibly know all the intricacies of the biometric system. Thus, a support point within the vendor's company needs to be identified. By this point, the company should have entered into a service level agreement with the vendor for support. At this level of internal support, the company's support personnel need direct access to a live person at the vendor's help desk. This will ensure timely answers to questions and concerns.

- Changes made to standard configurations in support of the project—When the members of the production team were deploying the project, they may have made changes to the standard desktop builds. These changes need to be documented and articulated to the support group. When the support group gets a call for support, it needs to know what is different from the original specifications. The support group may need to re-install the desktop build or change it. By knowing what needs to be different to support the biometric system, additional user inconvenience can be avoided.

- What types of support activities may adversely affect the project?—It is good to know what standard support activities should be changed or avoided when supporting the biometric system. This could include actions like upgrading system files, disabling particular drivers or services, or applying particular patches or service packs. Any inconsistency needs to be documented. At the same time, the minimum and optimum system requirements need to be clear. That way, if software or hardware needs to be changed, the support team can make sure the minimum system requirements are still being met.

Why Is This Chapter So Short?

By the time a project reaches the rollout stage, all the prerequisite work should have been done. That means the only thing left to do is deploy the rollout. By this time, the project plan has been modified and a deployment schedule has been created. These are the only two documents you need to get the deployment done. Lastly, the only document to be produced from this part of the project is the transition book for support. So relax! All the hard work has been done and everything will go very smoothly!

Conclusion

The rollout is when all the previous hard work pays off. It shows that the company has invested the necessary time and money to bring the project to this stage. All that is left to do is get the hardware and software deployed. The speed at which deployment happens is generally slowly at the start, so as to build on initial successes and momentum. It is better to walk out of the starting blocks than to sprint out and trip on your own feet! At the same time, the deployment schedule must be attainable; now is not the time for schedule and/or cost over-runs. Make sure the support infrastructure is ready for the go-live day and the support agreement is in place for the company. Lastly, make sure a support transition book is created and handed off to support.

Part 4

FUTURE AND CONCLUSIONS

15

The Future
of Biometric
Authentication

The future of any technology is difficult to predict. Biometric authentication is a field that is making rapid advances. The use of new materials for imaging biometrics and the development of new types of biometrics will continue. Below are some areas I am willing to speculate about as I gaze into the future:

Will Biometrics Be Integrated Everywhere?

While it is interesting to think that we can use biometrics for everything, the reality is less promising. Biometrics will continue to be adopted in both the logical and physical access worlds. The biometrics used for logical access will still need to be low in cost, high in user acceptance, and very easy to use. The biometric device will also need to have a small footprint on the desktop. This will limit these logical-access biometric devices to finger, hand, face, eye, and voice types. For physical access, the choice of biometrics will depend on their application. If it is a high-volume application, then an active biometric will need to be used, like face, voice, or gait. If the application has lower throughput requirements, then many of the same types of biometrics used for logical access will also apply.

As for one biometric itself becoming pervasive, that will depend on cost and user acceptance. Currently, the implementation of biometrics into devices like laptops and phones has not progressed at the rate anticipated. This is because of the low margins that are on these items. Just a fraction of an increase in cost can make their production unprofitable.

Thus, the price needs to come down. As for user acceptance, I think, like the telephone and the home computer, as a biometric device becomes more pervasive in people's working lives, the more likely they are to accept it in their personal lives. Still, there are technological and logistical hurdles to overcome. Imagine using an active biometric sensor at home; the children return home and use the sensor after playing in the dirt and mud all day. Imagine the family hopping into the car to go somewhere and Dad and Mom cannot get authenticated to start the car. We thought children asking "Are we there yet?" was annoying; what would happen if we could not even start the trip? Besides the technology hurdles, what would be the logistics of keeping our biometric enrollments current in all these different systems? It could become as bothersome as using passwords!

What I feel will get us closer to ubiquity is the use of personal authentication devices. These personal authentication devices would have our biometric traits enrolled and ready for verification. The on-board cryptographic store would contain digital signatures for things such as banking, commerce, physical access, logical access, and other personal uses. The personal authentication devices would communicate securely using Bluetooth wireless technology to other devices requesting authentication, and the types of certificates required for access would be given. In this way, we could have strong authentication and still keep the logistics manageable.

What Other Biometric Measures Will Exist?

As biometric technology advances, more exotic forms of measurement will become available. These new features could measure things like the electro-magnetic field of a person or the internal structure of the human body.

Current research in using Terrahertz wavelengths will allow for the internal viewing of bone and tissue structures. This would be a good biometric to use as it would be available while wearing protective suits and gloves, and could do very reliable alive-and-well detection on the users. It is also safe. This technology is being designed to use nano-technologies from the outset. As such, it will be easy to integrate into existing and future applications.

Research in reading electromagnetic patterns has been in development for a number of years. This technology comes from the use of space-based telescopes. Now the technology is being commercialized for use in other applications.

It is not hard to believe that any individual physical or psychological trait could one day be tapped for biometrics. Maybe someday they will be able to use the distinct patterns of brainwaves!

A Futuristic Example: New Form of "Caller ID"

The advent of caller ID on the phone has led to the ability to decide if you want to talk to someone or not. It also allows us to be identified when we call into utilities like the phone company for immediate account access. Caller ID still suffers from the fact that it is anonymous to a certain degree. While the name associated with a number can be displayed, there is no guarantee that the party on the other end is who the caller ID says it is. Enter the new age of biometrics. Caller ID could be supplemented with voice biometrics. That is, the display name would appear, and when the phone is answered and the calling party speaks, a positive identification could be made.

What if this concept of identifying who is calling could be taken into new contexts? Currently we are under constant surveillance. Every move we make and transaction we execute can be positively traced back to us. With the cost of biometric technology falling, it will soon be reliable and cheap enough for everyday use. For example:

- Enter your favorite coffee shop in the morning, and your coffee order is waiting for you at the counter.
- You walk past the suit shop and it calls out to you by name, saying the latest spring fashions are in.
- Your daughter's boyfriend, whom you do not like, comes to the house and the door won't open to let him in.
- Your own little personal identification device recognizes someone you have not seen in years and provides you with his/her name. This could result in no more embarrassing blank looks on your face!

While all the above increase our personal convenience, they could also prove to be privacy risks. For example:

- The coffee shop will find it easy to track your purchasing habits. It could, without your knowledge, sell that information to other marketing companies, or to your healthcare provider.
- The suit shop could sell your purchasing preferences to other retailers, along with your biometric data. Now, you would not be able to go anywhere without targeted advertising.
- Your daughter's privacy is invaded because you know how often her boyfriend comes over and, more importantly, at what times!
- Your personal authentication device could be subpoenaed by the police to prove your association with someone.

All these increases in convenience also come with possible losses of privacy. As such, stronger government regulations will be required to cover the use and correlation of biometric data to other data. This way, by safeguarding the public, biometric systems will be more widely adopted.

Conclusion

As with any technological advance, some form of government regulation will be needed to protect the privacy of citizens. With this new protection of personal data and the right to privacy, new uses for biometrics that will provide a more secure and convenient world will emerge. Biometric technology will continue to expand as the human quest for knowledge continues. Sometimes the leap in technology will be large; at other times, only small amounts of progress will be made. Either way, the field of biometrics will continue, and its use and applicability will increase as well.

Glossary

ACL (Access Control List)   A table of access rights for a user to a particular file or other networked resource.

Active biometric   A biometric to which the user must actively submit a physical trait for measurement.

AFIS (Automated Fingerprint Identification System)   AFIS is a system to automatically match and classify fingerprints. Originally developed by the Federal Bureau of Investigations, it is now used by many law enforcement groups.

Algorithm   A step-by-step method of problem-solving that is predictable and reproducible.

ANN (Artificial Neural Network)   The Artificial Neural Network is a series of algorithms, assumptions, and probabilities used to solve a problem by simulating the operation of the human brain.

ArcNet   A LAN technology that uses virtual token-passing as a means of communicating on a shared network.

Authentication   The process of determining if a person is who he/she claims to be.

Binning   The process of presorting biometric data to make matching more accurate and quicker.

Biometric   A physical trait that can be measured and used for authentication.

Bleeding edge   The part of the life cycle of a product or market segment that is at the earliest stage of use and testing. This stage is found before the leading edge of a technology that is beginning to mature.

Brute force   The energy exerted in testing all possible outcomes in order to find a solution to a problem.

BSC (Binary Synchronous Communications)   A character-oriented synchronous link communications protocol evolved from the old asynchronous (start-stop) protocol. Originated by IBM in 1964.

Capacitance   The measure of capacitance is equal to the ratio of the charge on either surface (in a capacitor) to the potential difference between the surfaces (of a capacitor).

Capture   To gather the biometric trait to be measured.

CCD (Charge Coupled Device)   Is a light-sensitive integrated circuit that stores and displays the data for an image in such a way that each pixel (picture element) in the image is converted into an electrical charge the intensity of which is related to a color in the color spectrum. A CCD is a highly specialized integrated circuit that consumes more power then a CMOS device, but offers higher quality images.

certis paribus   Latin for "all other things being equal."

CMOS (Complementary Metal-Oxide Semiconductor)   Is a light-sensitive integrated circuit that stores and displays the data for an image in such a way that each pixel (picture element) in the image is converted into an electrical charge the intensity of which is related to a color in the color spectrum. Unlike a CCD, it is produced using standard chip manufacturing techniques and consumes lower power then a CCD.

CRL (Certificate Revocation List)   A list of certificates published by a certificate authority that have been revoked.

DHCP (Dynamic Host Configuration Protocol)   A protocol to dynamically configure the TCP/IP settings of a workstation or networked device.

Economies of scale   Getting a larger return on money spent by having a larger number of similar items in use.

EEPROM (Electronic Erasable Programmable Read-Only Memory)   A programmable read-only memory module that can be reprogrammed by applying a sufficiently large enough current to the memory.

EER (Equal Error Rate)   A measure of where the FAR and FRR curves intersect. It is used to measure the strength of a biometric algorithm.

Eigenface   A method of representing a human face as a linear deviation from a mean or average face.

EMF (Electromagnetic Frequency)   The generalized term for light and radio waves transmitted through space.

ENA (Extended Network Addressing)   A feature of SNA that enables the construction of extremely large (up to 8 million Logical Units (LUs) and 255 subnets) networks.

Enrollment   The act of capturing and indoctrinating a user into a biometric system.

FAR (False Acceptance Rate)   The probability that a biometric system will incorrectly identify an individual or will fail to reject an imposter.

Floppy   A portable magnetic disk medium used to store and transfer computer data from one machine to another. Originally called a floppy because the disk casing itself was flexible.

FMR (False Match Rate)   Equivalent to FAR.

FNMR (False Non-Match Rate)   Equivalent to FRR.

FRR (False Rejection Rate)   The probability that a biometric system will fail to identify an enrollee, or verify the legitimate claimed identity of an enrollee.

FTE (Failure to Enroll)   Failure of the biometric system to form a proper enrolment template for an end-user.

FUD (Fear, Uncertainty, and Doubt)   A term used to describe an environment of confusion or indecisiveness caused by providing future-based statements, or information that is provided only to further confuse a situation.

GINA (Graphical Identification and Authentication)   A Microsoft technology used to authenticate a user.

Identification   Finding out who someone is without that person's making a claim about his/her identity. Normally done using a one-to-many match of biometric templates.

IPX (Internetwork Packet Exchange)   A networking protocol from Novell that interconnects networks that use Novell's NetWare clients and servers. IPX is a datagram or packet protocol.

Jack in   To connect to a network.

Killer application   The application that makes a new technology worthwhile. For the personal computer, the killer application was a spreadsheet program called Lotus 123.

LAN (Local Area Network)   A group of computers and associated devices that share a common communications line.

Latent print   A fingerprint that has been left behind after touching an object.

LDAP (Lightweight Directory Access Protocol)   Is a software protocol for enabling anyone to locate organizations, individuals, and other resources such as files and devices in a network, whether on the public Internet or on a corporate intranet.

Leading edge   A point in a product's market maturity that has the early adopters trying out the technology for features and applicability.

LED (Light-Emitting Diode)   A semiconductor device that emits visible light when an electric current passes through it.

Live template   A biometric template created for matching to a previously enrolled biometric trait.

Minutia   Small details found in finger images such as ridge endings or bifurcations.

MOC (Match on Card)   Using a smart card to run a biometric matching algorithm on its own processor.

Multi-factor authentication   Using more than one factor of authentication at a time. For example, a biometric and token used together are considered multi-factor authentication.

NetBEUI (NetBIOS Extended User Interface)   Is a new, extended version of Net-BIOS, the program that lets computers communicate within a local area network. NetBEUI (pronounced net-BOO-ee) formalizes the frame format (or arrangement of information in a data transmission) that was not specified as part of NetBIOS. NetBEUI was developed by IBM for its LAN Manager product and has been adopted by Microsoft.

Non-repudiation   Being unable to deny executing a transaction.

One-to-one   A type of matching normally done for verification where a statement of identity is confirmed using only one of the biometric templates of the identity being claimed.

One-to-many   A type of matching normally done for identification where a statement of identity is not made. The live template is compared against all the stored templates in the biometric system.

One-way hash   An algorithm that turns messages or text into a fixed string of digits, usually for security or data management purposes. The "one-way" means that it's nearly impossible to derive the original text from the string.

Passive biometric   A type of biometric device or system that can capture biometric traits without the subject's submitting to the measurement.

Password   A secret string of characters that is used to prove one's identity to a computer system.

PCB (Printed Circuit Board)   A computer component board that has etched or printed pathways for interconnecting the components to be placed on the board.

PIN (Personal Identification Number)   Normally a secret code composed mainly of numbers.

PKI (Public Key Infrastructure)   Enables users of an otherwise insecure public network such as the Internet to securely and privately exchange data through the use of a public and a private cryptographic key pair. Public keys may be obtained and shared through a trusted authority.

Proxy   To execute a transaction or provide data on behalf of another.

ROC (Receiver Operator Curve)   A graph showing how the FRR and FAR vary according to the threshold.

ROI (Return on Investment)   The amount of money saved or earned based on the outlay of initial funds.

Smart card   A small computing processor affixed to a sheet of plastic the size of a credit or bank card. It is used either to store value or for the storage and retrieval of user data.

SNA (Systems Network Architecture)   IBM's data communications architecture defining levels of protocols for communications between terminals and applications, and between programs.

Snake oil   A euphemism for a product or service that is sold for more than what it is. Normally associated with exaggerated claims for performance.

Sneaker-net A method of sharing data among un-networked computers by carrying a portable storage medium to the next computer.

SPX (Sequenced Packet Exchange) A transport-layer protocol built on top of IPX. SPX is used in Novell NetWare systems for communications in client/server application programs.

SSL (Secure Sockets Layer) A commonly used protocol for managing the security of a message transmission on the Internet.

SSO (Single Sign-On) A user authentication process that permits a user to enter one name and password to access multiple applications or resources.

Stored template A previously enrolled template that is used for comparison against a live template.

TCP/IP (Transmission Control Protocol/Internet Protocol) A combination of two protocols that describes how data is delivered and networked resources are addressed.

Template A mathematical representation of a physical biometric trait. It is not the raw stored data of the original biometric trait.

Type I error In statistics, the rejection of the null hypothesis (default assumption) when it is true. In a biometric system, the usual default assumption is that the claimant is genuine, in which case, this error corresponds to a "False Rejection".

Type II error In statistics, the acceptance of the null hypothesis (default assumption) when it is false. In a biometric system, the usual default assumption is that the claimant is genuine, in which case, this error corresponds to a "False Acceptance".

USB (Universal Serial Bus) A plug-and-play interface between a computer and add-on devices.

Verification The process of comparing a submitted biometric sample against the biometric reference template of a single enrollee whose identity is being claimed, to determine whether it matches the enrollee's template.

x.500 A standard way to develop an electronic directory of people in an organization so that it can be part of a global directory available to anyone in the world with Internet access.

XOR (eXclusive OR) Is a mathematical function with two inputs. If the two inputs are the same, the output is a 0, or if the inputs are different, the output is a 1.

Bibliography

1. AuthenTec, Inc. "Fingerprint Matching Technology–The Basics," June 7, 2002 (www.authentec.com/finalInteg/MatchingBasics_files/frame.htm).

2. AuthenTec, Inc. "Operating Principles for Very Small Fingerprint Sensors," June 7, 2002 (www.authentec.com/finalInteg/HowSmallSensorsWork_files/frame.htm).

3. AuthenTec, Inc. "Specifying Commercial and Consumer Fingerprint Systems," June 7, 2002 (www.authentec.com/finalInteg/SpecComFprintSyst_files/frame.htm).

4. AuthenTec, Inc. "TruePrint Technology–The Fundamentals," June 7, 2002 (www.authentec.com/finalInteg/TechieDetail_files/frame.htm).

5. Bishop, Peter. "Atmel's Fingerchip Technology for Biometric Security," November 2002 (www.atmel.com).

6. Bromba, Manfred. "Bioidentification," September 12, 2003 (www.bromba.com).

7. Broun, C.C., X. Zhang, R.M. Mersereau, and M. Clements. "Automatic Speechreading with Application to Speaker Verification," (www.users.ece.gatech.edu).

8. Bruderlin, Rene. "What Is Biometrics? Automated Identification of Persons based on Personal Characteristics," 2001 (www.bioservice.ch).

9. Daugman, John. "How Iris Recognition Works," University of Cambridge (www.cl.cam.ac.uk/users/jgd1000).

10. Davies, Simon G. "Touching Big Brother: How Biometric Technology Will Fuse Flesh and Machine," *Information Technology & People*, Vol. 7, No. 4, 1994.

11. de Boer, Johan, Asker M. Bazen, and Sabih H. Gerez. "Indexing Fingerprint Databases Based on Multiple Features" (www.stw.nl.prorisc/proc2000).

12. Dugelay, J.L., J.C. Junqua, C. Kptropoulos, R. Kuhn, F. Perronnin, and I. Pitas. "Recent Advances in Biometric Person Authentication," (www.eurecom.fr/~perronni/papers/icassp02.pdf).

13. Dunlap, Duane D. November 2001 (http://et.wcu.edu/aidc/).

14. Ernst, Jan. "Iris Recognition and Identification," December 2, 2002 (www.iris-recognition.org).

15. Ethentica. "Tactilesense White Paper A Breakthrough in Fingerprint Authentication," January 2003 (www.securityfirstcorp.com/tactwhtpr.pdf).

16. Frischholz, Robert. "Face Detection," August 29, 2003 (www.home.tonline.de/home/RobertFrischholz/face/htm).

17. Ganger, Gregory R. and David F. Nagle. "Better Security via Smarter Devices," May 2001 (www.pdl.cs.cmu.edu/PDL-FTP/Secure/hotos01.pdf).

18. Govindavajhala, Sudhakar, and Andrew W. Appel, "Using Memory Errors to Attack a Virtual Machine," Dept. of Computer Science, Princeton University, Princeton, NJ, 2003.

19. Harper, Jim. "Biometrics: New Weapons in the War Against Terrorism or New Blow to Privacy?" Prepared Remarks to the American Bar Association Section of Science and Technology Law Panel, August 11, 2002.

20. Harris, Tom. "How Fingerprint Scanners Work," 2003 (www.computer.howstuffworks.com).

21. Hawkins, Dana. "Who's Watching Now? Hassled by Lawsuits, Firms Probe Workers' Privacy," *U.S. News*, September 15, 1997.

22. Infineon. (www.infineon.com/cmc_upload/documents/028/946/FREQUENTLYASKEDQUESTIONS.pdf).

23. Jain, Anil K. and Sharath Prabhakar. "Fingerprint Classification and Matching," (www.research.ibm.com/ecvg/pubs/sharat-handbook.pdf).

24. Jain, Anil K., S. Prabhakar, and Arun Ross. "Fingerprint Matching: Data Acquisition and Performance Evaluation," March 1999 (www.cse.msu.edu/cgi-user/web/tech/document?ID=402).

25. Kingpin. "Attacks on and Countermeasures for USB Hardware Token Devices," 2002 (www.atstake.com).

26. Leeper, David, Jeff Foerster, Evan Green, and Srinivasa Somayazulu. *Secure Solutions*, May 3, 2002 (www.digitalpersona.com).

27. Lewis, Peter. "Verizon sues State over Rules on Privacy," *Seattle-Times*, November 22, 2002.

28. Liedy, Martin V. "Biometric Security Systems the Next Generation of Security."

29. Mansfield, A.J., and J.L. Wayman. "Best Practices in Testing and Reporting Performance of Biometric Devices," Version 2.01, August 2002 (www.cesg.gov.uk/site/ast/biometrics).

30. Marinov, Svetoslav. "Text Dependent and Text Independent Speaker Verification Systems, Technology and Applications," February 26, 2003 (www.speech.kth.se).

31. Mast, Lucas. "Biometrics: Hold On, Chicken Little," *TechKnowledge*, No. 31, January 18, 2002.

32. Matsumoto, Tsutomu. "Importance of Open Discussion on Adversarial Analyses for Mobile Security Technologies—A Case Study for User Identification," May 14, 2002 (www.itu.int/itudoc/itu-t/workshop/security/present/s5p4.pdf).

33. May, Timothy C. "The Cyphernomicon: Cypherpunks FAQ and More," Version 0.666, September 10, 1994 (www.www2.pro-ns.net/crypto).

34. MIT Media Laboratory Vision and Modeling Group Face Recognition Demo Page, July 25, 2002 (www.whitechapel.media.mit.edu).

35. Pankanti, Sharath, Salil Prabhakar, and Anil K. Jain. *On The Individuality of Fingerprints*, Michigan State University, 2001.

36. Penzhorn, W.T. "Principles of Network Security Lecture N-03 Biometric User Identification" (www.ict.tuwein.ac.at/skripten/Penzhorn).

37. Schuckers, Stephanie, Larry Hornak, Tim Norman, Reza Derakhshani, and Sujan Parthasaradhi. "Issues for Liveness Detection in Biometrics" (www.biometrics.org/html/bc2002_sept_program/2_bc0130_DerakhshabiBrief.pdf).

38. Shankar, Asim, and Priyendra Singh Deshwal. *Face Detection in Images: Neural Networks & Support Vector Machines,* Indian Institute of Technology at Kanpur, April 2002.

39. Shinn, Phil. "Speaker Verification," Telephony Voice User Interface Conference, Scottsdale, AZ, January 1999.

40. Singer, Brooke. *Against Data Determinism in a Networked World,* Spring 2002 (www.bsing.net).

41. Speir, Michelle. "The New Face of Security: Understanding the Promises and Pitfalls of Facial-Recognition Technology," March 4, 2002 (www.iwsinc.com).

42. Suares, Stuart. "Biometric Security Systems" (www.biometricsecurity.com.au/technologies).

43. Thompson, Susan. "Improving Biometrics" (www.silicontrust.com/pdf/secure_5/50_techno_5.pdf).

44. Visualize. "Face Recognition: A camera and Algorithm Know It's You," November 2001 (www.technologyreview.com).

45. Wayman, James L. "Biometric Identification Standards Research Final Report, Volume I," San Jose State University, December 1997.

46. Woodward, John D., Katharine W. Webb, Elaine M. Newton, Melissa Bradley, and David Rubenson. *Army Biometric Applications: Identifying and Addressing Sociocultural Concerns,* Rand Corporation, 2001.

47. Wrigley, Stuart N. "Speech Recognition by Dynamic Time Warping," 1999.

Index

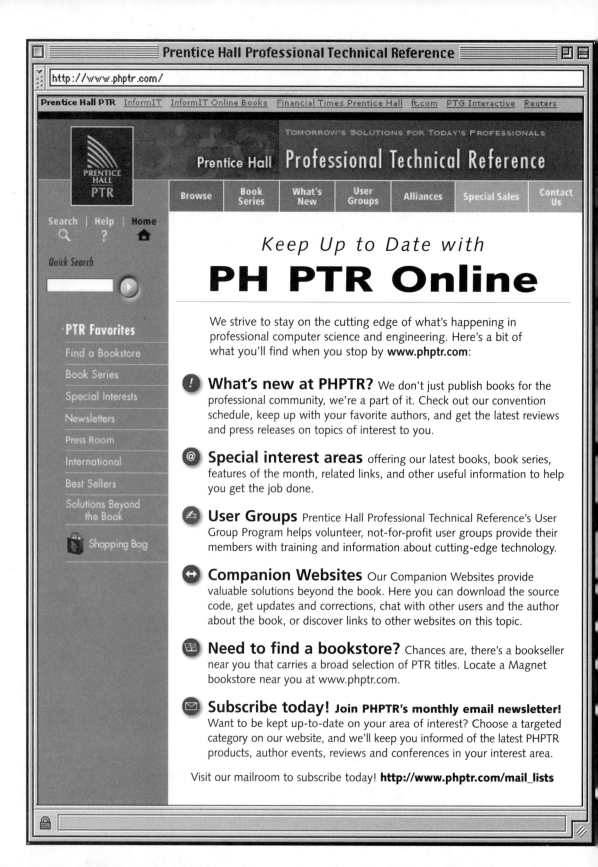